# *Poetry in a Pandemic*

DAILY MUSINGS FOR A WORLD IN TURMOIL

H. M. GOODEN

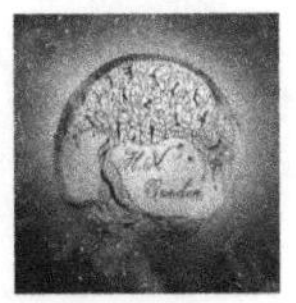

# Foreword

When I initially came up with the idea of compiling my daily poetry practice into a book, I thought I'd start with the pandemic.

It was, and still is, an important moment in history, and I wanted a way to look back and remember where I was and what I was thinking at a time when life was changing dramatically.

But then I paused.

I'd begun keeping a daily blog in 2016 as a way to add more creativity to life after the birth of my last child, and one of the ways I kept it going was by challenging myself to write every day for a year—just to see if I could.

When I succeeded, I'd slowly lapsed into occasional writing. As the gaps in entries grew larger, I missed it enough to resurrect it again in December of 2019.

But as any horror or paranormal stories have shown us over the years, when you bring something back from the dead, it's never quite the same as it was before.

This reincarnation may have started with the same intention, but the blog quickly became something different as days passed.

The December entries are serious, leading with a piece

from December 6th on the anniversary of the École Polytechnic murders in Montréal, but over time they transform into more of a gratitude practice.

Then I let my natural love of word play take over and allowed myself rhyme, even though I'd always felt rhyming was not "cool" anymore. (Aren't "real" poets supposed to be esoteric and broody types?)

So what changed?

Maybe because I found a groove, but if I'm honest with myself, it was likely more the passage of time. The world is a hard place for everyone at least occasionally, and I didn't want more hard in my life.

I wanted play. I wanted gratitude.

And, most of all, I wanted magic, both in my fiction and my nonfiction.

I wanted to celebrate life, the universe in all its imperfections, and wanted to bring beauty and magic into other people's lives as well.

Because if it's true we become what we focus on and head where we set our sights, why not point our ships to the stars?

Why not spend more time believing in the good in the world, and try to multiply that instead of the bad?

What do we have to lose but negativity?

In this thirteen month selection of my life, I hope some of my longing for *more* comes through. I hope you reach for this book and feel better every time you visit, even if you only read one page a day.

After all, it took me that long to write it.

With love and possibilities,

H. M. Gooden

CHAPTER ONE

# December 2019

December 6th, 2019

I miss having a daily blog.

2019 proved challenging in many ways. Maintaining regular posts of any form disappeared somewhere on the way to December without notice but, when I finally came up for air, I couldn't help but feel the lack.

Sure, I could blame not writing daily updates on the time I spent working on other writing projects, many which led me down deep rabbit holes of editing and deadlines, but the truth is I simply didn't prioritize it the way it needed to be.

I didn't know how much I depended on daily word prompts from Twitter to spark something for me to write about until they no longer arrived in my mailbox in the spring of 2019.

Between the missing prompts and my personal challenge to blog every day coming to an end in 2018, it proved to be another (nearly final) nail in the coffin of the habits I'd developed over the previous two years.

As things do, the days got busy, my focus changed, and the usual excuses popped up as other goals took priority.

Now, as the holiday season looms once again, I'm feeling nostalgic for what was.

Nostalgia is a lovely and fickle creature, but this time she brought me a realization I decided to use to my advantage. My daily blog, Thought Salad, had added value to my days by providing a regular time where I stopped to pause and reflect.

I knew I wanted Thought Salad in my life, and that's why I'm starting it again, today. I could wait for New Year's and make it part of a resolution, but why? I'm a bit of a rebel when it comes to things like that anyway, and I'd rather work on a time line that uses my current motivation to jump start a new habit.

And in addition to that came a reminder of what day today is. December $6^{th}$.

The anniversary of the massacre of fourteen young, vibrant, intelligent women at École Polytechnique in Montréal, Canada. A day I still remember, even though I was only eleven at the time because I couldn't understand why anyone would even consider doing such a thing.

On Dec $6^{th}$, 1989, fourteen women with their entire lives ahead of them were brutally murdered, in cold blood, in a classroom in Canada.

A country that prides itself on fairness, hockey, good coffee, and beer.

A country that has no significant history of gun violence, with strict rules and regulations around who can purchase and carry weapons.

The original reports skirted the issue, downplaying the circumstances leading to the tragedy.

"An angry man"

"A sick individual."

Today, there is no doubt what led to this unthinkable attack.

Misogyny.

The societal acceptance of violence against women, and a specific, targeted attack against feminists. Because to the man who carried out this atrocity, the women attending that program counted as feminist simply by virtue of working toward higher education.

They were stepping out of what was "nice" and doing what they wanted to with their lives, not what someone else thought they should. They were enrolled in Engineering Sciences, a "male" area of study women have traditionally been discouraged from showing an interest in.

It was thirty years ago today, yet I can't help wondering how far we've come as a society in terms of equality.

Women are still disproportionately likely to suffer violence perpetrated by both strangers and loved ones.

One woman in Canada dies every day.

Once a week the murderer is someone they love.

Women make less money for the same work.

Two in ten women are sexually harassed in the work place.

I have been.

Multiple times.

But you carry on.

Because what else can you do?

Because we are used to the world being like this.

Because it isn't surprising. Sad, yes, but surprising, no.

A colleague of mine posted a wonderful, thoughtful article about why so many women are uncomfortable having a pelvic exam performed by a male physician.

The replies were deafening, and heartbreaking.

People were calling it reverse sexism and saying it has to stop. But it is not reverse sexism when you are worried someone will hurt you because you have already been hurt.

STOP BLAMING THE VICTIM AND START SEEING THE PROBLEM!

It makes everyone—men and women—uncomfortable to admit the world is not fair.

But it isn't fair.

It isn't equal.

(I won't go into all the ways, because I still have to go to work today. Please believe me when I say I understand I am barely scratching the surface on the many ways this world is not equal)

Women are every bit as likely to support the status quo as men, don't kid yourself. Maybe it's because they don't want to cause waves, or they're scared, or for as many reasons as there are people.

Men often do not see it when it doesn't affect them, but sometimes, it's because they are afraid too.

What would the world look like if one day we all did wake up and change?

I truly believe most people are good.

I think we all want to live in a world where people get along and are safe to live happy, fulfilling, and productive lives where everyone has a chance to create something amazing.

Today will always be a reminder for me of how far we still have to go. Until we live in a society where everyone is equal, we have work to do. And until that day arrives, there's always room for self reflection.

My goal is to be part of the solution instead of part of the problem.

In 2020, I plan to see more clearly and act more boldly.

What about you?

## December 7th

### Little Man

twinkle, twinkle
little child
you are fast
and oh, so wild
right beside my heart you sleep
dreaming of oceans,
blue, and deep
when the morn arrives again
you'll tell me stories
of sun and rain
my littlest,
but not at all the least
my funny,
happy,
little beast

## December 8th

### Monsters

I used to believe
(when I was a child)
in witches and werewolves
and evil so wild
back then, things went bump in the night
but now that I'm grown
the monsters are bright
they wear the faces of people
who seem innocent and kind
and it's harder to know
what goes on inside their mind
when the light of the day
doesn't make the demons run
wolf wear sheep's clothing
and get to have fun
so keep your eyes open;
the danger is real
walking amongst us
waiting for it's next meal

## December 9th

### High waters

Today started far too early.

I woke before the dawn, unable to still my racing thoughts. Monday is often a struggle, especially with too little sleep to help start the day. But even though my list of things to do is relatively short, I'm left somehow bereft and feeling at sea with myself.

Like a victim of a shipwreck, I hold onto a stray board and wonder how I got there. The waves are too high, submerging me and making me choke.

But then, just when I learn how to swim and keep my head above water, the surf goes out, and I'm left beached and gasping in the sun. The calm somehow even more frightening than the cyclone which preceded it.

There's a different kind of storm brewing now, one I'm not sure I know how to weather, but I can feel it coming.

For now, I'll keep doing what I can to tread water, moving forward as I search the horizon for a boat or sandy beach.

Maybe I'll find a safe place to rest awhile before continuing on my way, kicking and paddling until I reach my harbour, come hell or high water.

Sometimes, the only way to make it through the waves is to wait in the center of the storm until it's over.

## December 10th

### Precipice of Night

sleep is here again
soft breathing
where moments earlier
kids played
"Just one more"
"I'm not that tired"
"But why do THEY get to stay?"
silence surrounds me
now interrupted only by
a black cat purring
and the gentle thump
of a heartbeat next to mine
peace expands,
my eyelids
weighed down by the day
now only a blurred memory
as I float off to restore my soul
from the Well of Dreams

## December 11th

### The Christmas Concert

they stood up front,
smiling with rouged cheeks
and painted on noses
the reindeers and elves,
Santa, and Mrs. Claus, too
singing their hearts out,
shining like the diamonds
they are to me and to you,
bouncing with pride
when they see
their loved ones in the crowd
then cookies and the recap
another year's tradition
accomplished with delight

## December 12th

### A Blessing of Brownies

a hailstorm of holidays,
a blessing of brownies
crafting by the dozen
turns frowns upside-downies
when Santa arrives
everyone loudly cheers
and carols are sung
without regard for adult ears
another late night
but that's quite okay
because Christmas is here
in just a few days
I'm ready for sleep
even if the children are not
at least we'll go to bed happy
with cookies,
hugs,
and the lot

## December 13th

### Clarity

disappointment
is the distance
between
expectations
and reality
Clarity
is knowing
we can decide
how far
that distance
will be

## December 14th

### Family and Friends

It's a later night than usual, but I'm still wide awake, thinking about my day.

Possibly some of my alertness is due to the coffee I partook in, along with several overly decadent Nanaimo squares. Both my stomach and head are buzzing right now, but I think the main reason I'm still awake is because of how full my heart is (and yes, okay, my stomach too! )

I've had a day full of more human interaction without expectation than I've had in a long time. Time with my children, my husband, and friends, time to think, breathe, and laugh.

It's funny how fast a day goes by when you spend it with those you love.

And though I'm far past my bedtime, I know my dreams will be restful.

With my spirit so fully replenished, I may even sleep past six am.

## December 15th

### Love

petal soft
the rose
is held aloft
by hands
tender
and strong
the fragrance of home
memories of love
eternal summer
blooms

## December 16th

### Mixed Metaphors

The start of another week has arrived; one week closer to the holidays. My children are nearly dancing at breakfast, eager for their upcoming break. Or, perhaps it's the thought of presents making them wiggle in their chairs?

I've chosen to spend my rare free moments the last few weeks of 2019 thinking about the direction I want my life to take in the year ahead.

While I love to plan, the truth is when I don't, it feels like things escape me, or worse, pull me along behind them like a waterskier dragged behind the wake of life, holding on the rope as the days speed past me without my consent.

This year, I want to be the one driving the boat, creating the waves that normally swamp me when the wind gets high.

I want to choose what to add in, what to take away, and figure out a way to create value where distractions usually chip away at my calm.

Ah, if only we got what we wished for!

But as they say, "if wishes were horses, then beggars would ride."

When I was a child, the saying made no sense to me. Why would a beggar want a horse?

But now that I'm an adult, I understand what my grandmother meant. I try to argue with reality, telling myself I'm not asking for a unicorn, or even a horse.

I'm simply asking for two short weeks to close my eyes and think about what's important. I want to make sure I'm using my 20/20 vision to see my goals clearly, not simply wish away the time, or worse, letting it drag me behind it, screaming all the way.

We all have the same twenty-four hours in a day, after all.

If an ounce of prevention is worth a pound of cure, then surely, two weeks can buy me a few months?

I guess only time will tell!

## December 17th

### Little Boy

infectious energy
aimed at all he sees
so hard to tell him no
he gets away
with everything
as he twinkles
from head to toe
he's a stinker
our little Matt
(but not like Mr. Grinch)
he jumps across
all the miles
if given half an inch
and even the day's daily work
when he snuggles close to me
the cares of my day evaporate
as his laughter sets me free

## December 18th

### Death and the Mother

Death came for her that morning,
and was greeted like a friend
old beyond her years,
broken long before her time
he'd gone on ahead to forge a path
he'd cared for her,
loved her for always,
as long as she's living,
her baby,
he'd been
but time was unkind
illnesses piled up and soon
weighed heavy on them both
a dutiful son,
he did what dutiful sons do
and traveling on ahead,
ensured her road was smooth
we never spoke his name,
nor told her of his passing
yet somehow,
even in the thickness
of her confusion she knew
unable to voice her grief
her actions shouted her pain to the roof
when I got that call in the night I knew too
eternally young they embraced again,
each made brand-new

## December 19th

### Chocolate Christmas Blues

too much chocolate,
cookies,
and treats
make me feel worse
the more I eat
I regret them before
I even finish chewing
but saying I'm not going
to have more is easier
than the actual doing
maybe after Christmas
I'll be back on the wagon
but right now,
send help,
my willpower's sagging!

## December 20th

### First Love

The sound of sobbing greeted my ears.

In the darkness, at first I thought I was dreaming. But then I saw them, crying at the side of my bed as if their heart was breaking.

Their most beloved had left them alone, to sleep without the warmth of companionship.

Even as I held him, rubbing his back while smoothing tears away, my heart warmed at the tender creature I'd been privileged to have given birth to.

Just when I thought my efforts in vain, they smiled and agreed it *was* very late, and tomorrow would be better. Because it's true; a cat will never stay when they have better things to do.

I tucked them back in, squeezing them once more. Smiling, I turned off the light and blew him a kiss.

My eyes filled by the sight of my little cat whisperer, my tiny double, snuggled into bed at peace once more.

## December 21st

### Imposter

some days you're flying
on the top of the world,
other days you're waiting
to be led away in chains
what if they knew everything?
would they believe in me
more than I do?
or would the opposite be true?
would they look at me,
frown and turn away,
wondering how they ever
made such a mistake
confusing me for someone else
someone smarter,
someone wiser,
someone taller,
someone brighter
each day I choose to think everyone
is doing their best in that moment
and yet I wonder
am I?
should I,
could I,
would I?
if I knew more,
could I be more?
am I living up to the impossible dream,
the one Don Quixote dared to dream?
or am I taking the easy way out
by saying I don't know
like a child caught with a hand in the cookie jar

the Dunning Kruger effect strikes me as odd,
funny
for if it's true,
I'm being absurd
and must know much more than I think I do
and if it's false,
perhaps it's the world I see that's wrong
regardless of the facts,
so I'll do what I do every day
continue about completing my tasks,
hoping no one discovers
the imposter in their midst

## December 22nd

Darkness and Light
neither can exist
without the night
and the day
to light the way
both within,
always without
to cast away one
is to let in the doubt
breathe in the air
exhale the earth
sister and brothers
death after birth
endless the loop
of laughter and pain
grief and suffering
humour and gain
to live without one
is to exist without
accept what isn't
and rise above doubt

## December 24th

### Christmas Eve

on the eve of Christmas
kids gather 'round
excitement overwhelms them,
they simply can't calm down
because they're expecting a visitor,
one who drives a cool sleigh
who brings so many toys
they can't wait to play
but as excited as they feel
they go to bed without fuss
because they know Santa's coming
to each one of us

## December 25th

It's Christmas morning and the fireplace is on.

The presents are nestled under the tree, stockings are hung by the fire with care (and nails, likely more than required, but those suckers aren't going anywhere, not on my husband's watch. No sir!)

The warmth that fills me even though it is only five in the morning is far beyond what a fireplace can provide. I love our new house. It's cozy, and perfect for us. I'm sitting alone and savouring the silence while the kids are in bed.

Right now, there's only a sense of peace in these still moments of dawn, the brief slivers of time between sleep and awake, before night gives over to day.

These moments won't last, but that's why I find them so precious. The more rare the jewel, the more one covets it.

Perhaps that's why friends and family are so often taken for granted by those lucky enough to have them in abundance.

But this year, I'm counting my blessings instead of presents, awed by my love for each one of them. That, more than anything else, is the true magic of Christmas.

Merry Christmas everyone. Thank you for being a part of my life.

## December 26th

The day after Christmas is often a let down, but this year our plans kept us ramped up. We were going on our fun family vacation, just because we wanted to.

The kids could hardly wait while we packed, almost equivalently excited as they were the night Santa was on his way. Then, after a long drive we reached our hotel.

It was just across the street from the West Edmonton Mall. We unpacked and ate before half of us decided to walk over for a little look-see and to get a little exercise for the ones who needed a good run.

But the unexpected hit us.

I was physically lifted, clinging to my oldest and youngest child's hands in shock.

It had been such an ordinary moment.

Just a truck deciding to turn right on a red. Somehow, they failed to see us crossing in the pedestrian corridor, with the little walking man lighting the way, while other people were walking through from the opposite direction.

With two screaming and crying kids, I failed to process my own pain and instead acted on a mother's instinct.

I got up as fast as I could, moving the oldest out of the road and onto the safety of the grassy shoulder, then turned to drag the small one out from under the tire of the truck.

I don't know how, but I pulled him out, all the while telling myself it's okay, it's just his leg, we've been through worse.

He'll be fine. It's just a leg.

He clung to me like a baby monkey, climbing higher as his tears tracked down his face and he howled his pain and shock, the way I wanted to wail but didn't.

Couldn't.

I was the mother, I had to be strong.

"I don't like that truck, it's a bad, bad truck!"

I calmed both children down as best as I could, got the driver to call 911 and called my husband.

The fire trucks came first, then the paramedics, and then finally, the police.

We took a ride to the hospital with nitrox for the pain, his leg splinted- crushed?- until we arrived.

We were ushered into the trauma room.

He was so brave, so funny on gas and novelty; learning the machine and the X-rays, making everyone laugh at chocolate being his favourite vegetable. (He is his daddy's boy!)

My relief at the normal imaging, even though he limped out, demanding to be carried because he was terrified to cross the road. Despite my previously unnoticed pain, I held him tight, carrying him every step of the way.

Keeping him safe.

Gratitude for all the staff and helpers along the way, for friends who stepped up to the plate, offered a bed and a shoulder.

When we returned back to the hotel room, we were greeted by three worried, wonderful faces.

Hopefully tomorrow, we will make better memories to replace the terror of today.

December 27th

Thoughts on the day after being hit by a truck .

So many new experiences this year, including many I would have been fine not having had at all. Some say you're never given more than you can handle—I, on the other hand, say that's a steaming pile of horse…hockey.

I see people given stuff they can't handle every day, things they should never have to handle. Sometimes they get through them, sometimes they can't. I'm not sure when it became popular to say this.

I'm even less sure when I started to say it to myself.

I do know that once again, I got "lucky" in my bad luck.

I can now boast of the dubious honour of saying I was hit by a truck and "you should see the other guy", or "I proved I'm built Ford Tough", but it's likely only funny in my head.

Also, Hollywood has super overestimated how easy it is to walk away from that. I came nowhere close to breaking the windshield and my left butt cheek is double the size of the right, not to mention the three different levels of bruises on my ankle, shin, and knees.

There's no way after experiencing the aftermath of that I will ever believe the hero in a movie is able to run away/after the bad guys.

Apparently, I may have blocked/punched/lifted the truck, as there is a bruise on my arm I don't remember getting and my wrist is swollen.

At least I can say I got some exercise yesterday after all?

The strange thoughts in my head are of course tempered by the sheer relief of watching my children have fun today. Sure, they were all up with nightmares last night, but so was I.

I rented a stroller for the little guy, which we wouldn't have done otherwise, but it was enough for him to limp off and on rides. Despite that, he had fun and everything else faded into the background, kind of like a movie that we saw once and went away.

Today, I'm working on finding the blessing and the life lesson in the random bad luck, and simply glad we're all here to appreciate it.

## December 29th

Small Picasso's
    working at their art
    each one unique
    although they share
    my heart

## December 30th

The end of the year is approaching,
faster than the speed of sound
as much as the winter is soft and white
still the snow lay on the ground
my emotions are jumping inside
with everything the year has brought
some days were glorious and special
Others were a little…fraught
but between the cares and worries
are marvellous moments I'll treasure
and as 2019 turns to the 20,
I'll hope, as always, for more leisure

## December 31st

May old acquaintance be forgot
and never brought to mind
even if it feels like yesterday
is no more than a step behind
another year is here again
and so the hourglass spins
ask anyone in the world
they'll say Father Time always wins
that's okay, I don't mind at all
I'm ready for the new
for along with this brand new year
I know I'll still have you

CHAPTER TWO

# January 2020

January 1st

New beginnings

The second day of January came in like a lion, making me wonder if the year was shaping up to be the one of clarity I'm craving so much.

Perhaps I became concerned about low visibility because of the blowing snow, but it the clincher was watching the Jeep a few cars ahead of me spin into the wrong lane of traffic.

Naturally I slowed down, but it reminded me of my life, and that in turn filled me with a strong sense of caution.

The last few months have been hard.

Beautiful and painful in equal measure, mixed up in a package so intense it makes me wonder how much more I can handle. Then in the next moment, I feel so blessed when I think about how much worse my life could be.

Have I been lucky?

I'm luckier than I deserve, and in so many ways.

I've gone years without significant badness happening, so perhaps it was just time for my pendulum to swing again.

But like everyone else, I don't care about all the good I've had.

I'm greedy and want more, but with none of the terrifying, earth-shaking, and potentially soul-crushing experiences to remind me that I, and everyone I love, are mere mortals after all.

No matter how much magic I dream of, create, or wish were real.

With these thoughts fresh in mind, I've decided the word I will focus on this year is Clairvoyant.

Using the original definition of the word, I want to be clear sighted this year: to accept the world as it is, but continue to do my best to work for the world as it could be.

To see my flaws and gifts equally and celebrate them each for making me unique.

To see those around me as the beautiful and unique humans they are, each worthy of love and kindness, and to be able to forgive them when they lash out in pain.

I want to see the beauty in nature and be able to stop in the middle of a bad day to look at the sharp blue sky against brilliant white snow and not feel the cold.

While I may have wished for magic powers as a child (and truthfully, I still do), I'm working toward living in the moment and most of all, being grateful for all of life's ups and downs.

## January 2nd

### At The Beginning, Again

surrounded by family and friends,
warm even in the snow
funny how fast
it all seems to go
close my eyes—
I'm only five
blink and then
I stand,
now thirty and ten
so far it's a journey
I'd trade for naught
not always easy,
even if well fought
time is as slippery
as the hills we slide on
but leaves us memories
daughters,
and sons

## January 3rd

### Anxiety

Frantic breathing
heart beat
jagged
wondering why
the edges
are ragged
panic rises
chases me
around
ties me in knots,
then kicks
while I'm down
inhale again
senses release
anxiety is such
a soul-crushing beast

### January 4th

My week off is almost over and I'm sad to see it go. If I'm being completely honest with myself, I did work half of it, but even that is such a change it feels like I've had an entire week of relaxation.

I cooked, cleaned, snuggled the kids, and throughout it all, still felt there was more I needed to catch up on.

Now, as I type this after watching three episodes of Witcher and crocheting two new scarves, I wonder why I work so much.

I could stay busy with my hobbies alone for the next forty years; fifty, if my eyes and hands hold out.

Contemplative again with the onset of a new year, I once again resolve to re-examine the treadmill I'm on and see clearly.

Priority means the first thing.

It isn't plural.

Perhaps if I repeat that enough times, I'll remember it one of these days.

## January 5th

This is the first time I'm posting about the platform I use to blog, and it's mostly because I'm confused by the recent weirdness and needed a place to complain about it.

Sometimes it won't post for days, while other times, it looks like it's posted six times.

Occasionally, it will use English to tell me why it hates me, but usually it's a string of error codes that mean nada to me.

Clearly, I have angered the small troll that runs the system.

If you see them, please let them know I am deeply sorry for any and all of my transgressions.

I've decided it's not them, it's me.

Well, actually, I decided that years ago, when I was using the ancient system PINE in university.

(Yes, I am that old.)

Pretty much from the time I got that first email account it was clear to me technology and I were not going to be simpatico.

(In grade six, I did learn how to program things into DOS. I even learned to make a turtle walk in it, so that's something, right?)

So, if my blog shows up a million times and it's repetitive, it's only partially my fault.

The rest is the troll's fault.

Take it up with them.

## January 6th

### Heartbreak

bruised and broken
lying on the ground
looking for solace
but there's none
to be found

## January 7th

I'm having a hard time falling asleep without hearing "Toss a coin to your Witcher" playing in my head.

I had the bare minimum of knowledge of the series prior to watching the Netflix original version of it (Thanks, Shauna Lee!) and I'm grateful for it, because it's helped me follow the rather confusing first few episodes.

(Mostly due to the time line, which plays a little fast and loose with things.)

And yet, despite that, I'm completely captivated.

It's been a long time since I've seen a show that made me not want to go read a book instead. The Witcher is a rousing success in that department, even if it is a little confusing.

(Sorry Cal Newport— learning about Deep Work isn't anywhere close to as exciting as watching Superman fight monsters. Just saying.)

Now, I'm alternating between impatience to find out what happens next and wondering if I'll ever write anything that good.

In the meanwhile, I'm going to toss a coin to my Witcher and see if he'll protect me from some zombies and stuff overnight.

See you when the season is over.

## January 8th

I'm tired.

The kind of tired you feel in your soul. You can't quite put your finger on it, but it's so heavy it's hard to get up.

Is it just January, falling hard?

Or something bigger?

Careening from work, to work, to more work, sometimes I wonder if or when I'll get a chance to rest.

Sit and smell the dirt and fresh grass of summer while light filters through the willows, making my hands look gilded, magical.

Where is the breeze that will lift my hair?

When can I close my eyes and feel like the fire-starter I used to be?

When they said you could be everything, I didn't realize it meant I'd have to *do* everything too.

At least being tired is good for sleeping.

Maybe that's part of my problem too.

Sleep is in short supply when aches and pains wake me up any time I lie down and rest more than six hours.

That's why for now, my best friends are the coffee in my cup that waits for me each morning, and the cat curled on my lap, demanding everything but expecting nothing.

Perhaps they've figured it out.

In my next forty years, I'll work harder at being more like my cat.

## January 9th

### Humane Society Brownies

Pussycat, pussycat
where are you?
Pitbull, oh pitbull,
you're pretty cute too
and the bunny
is adorable,
the turtle
so very funny
can I have a kitty?
or maybe a small little pup?
I promise to feed it
until it grows up
I'll volunteer to scoop poop,
and walk them, too
said every little girl
(and half their mommies, too)

## January 10th

### Road at my Back

I thought I was traveling
on the road
alone
miles from where I wanted to be
thousands more
from my home
but the wind
caressed my cheeks
and the sun
kissed my hair
nature
surrounded me
with tenderness and care

## January 11th

### Birthday Boy

my little boy,
no longer so little
he makes me smile
with his silly giggles
his words
may have gotten larger
but his grin
still outshines them all,
and each day
spent with him
is more brilliant
than the last

## January 12th

Another Sunday night,
contemplating the day,
thinking about the week ahead
What will it bring?
Death?
Life,
or change?
when each breath
could shape the world,
what should I do?
my children run free
while I clean up after them
wondering when it became my turn
to sit on the sidelines.
wondering
if it's too late
to run with them instead
a skip and a hop
gone again
Like whispers of smoke,
dissolving in the air

## January 13th

### Monday the 13th

"It's colder than a witches heart," I mutter, as I try to get warm for the ninetieth time today.

Glad to spend my time inside, I've worn slipper socks in my boots yet despite that, I had cold feet all day. If the saying, "cold hands, warm heart" is true, my heart must be the warmest one around.

I remember futile efforts to feel warm as a kid, and again as an adult. A brief interlude where I was too hot in pregnancy, and a short while after where being draped in small children was nice.

But the last two winters have stolen what little warmth was left in my body. Even the kids don't want to go outside, and when they do, I don't have to fight with them to get to zip up their jackets.

Only three more months to go until the sun wins out over Old Man winter. Until then, I'll bundle up and listen to the crunch of the snow beneath my boots, crisp and clean, and so very, very cold.

## January 14th

One month left until Valentine's Day.

I feel the love, even though the cold creeps into my fingers and toes, numbing and reminding me how glorious feeling warm is.

As I whine inside my head, I think of those who can't get warm.

Those with no home to go back to, no bed or cozy bodies to snuggle up to.

Those for whom the chill is more than bone deep, and has climbed into their souls.

My hands and toes may tingle, but the fire I have at home is built by those within its walls who wrap their love around me and hold me tight.

## January 15th

### Mountains

does it ever ask
if it's too high?
too sharp?
too mighty?
No.
it stands
proud,
confident in all it's glory
someday,
I'll be the one
standing strong;
a giant
against the wind

## January 16th

### Dusty

lounging
she stretches,
glorying in the carpet
Queen of all she surveys
content in her furry finery,
she accepts adoration
from the lesser creatures

## January 17th

Friday night

Falling into bed this Friday, I marvel at the changes the years have made. I've always loved early bedtimes, but now, snuggling in the warmth of the bed, with my kittens and kiddos around me, it's hard to concentrate.

My youngest plays his games while I read, but listening to him talk proves hard to ignore. Minecraft is beyond me, but clearly appeals to them, as they feed a pixelated cat while shooing away the IRL one who wants to lay on them.

I give up entirely, and learn more about the care and feeding of computer pets then I ever wanted to know, barely holding back a laugh at the serious discussion which ensues as his cat escapes.

Friday nights may not have the same kind of excitement they did twenty years ago, but I wouldn't trade them for the world.

## January 18th

### Saturday night in

It's hard to stay up past eight when it's so cozy in here.

Full of pancakes, we snuggle on the couch, watching some random cartoon movie.

Kids each tucked into "their" spot around the TV while a cat snoozes on the stairs.

But that's okay— there's nowhere else I'd rather be other than here, at home.

## January 19th

Another Sunday night
before the week begins;
a rush of sound and noise
I give thanks for all I have,
keeping close my memories of the week,
as close to me
as my girls and boys.

## January 20th

### Blue Monday

It's said that the third Monday of the year is the saddest.

"Blue Monday" is all I hear on the radio and TV right now.

While I may be bewildered at the speed time is passing, I'm not sad. It's February, with all its fake hearts and chocolates I find harder for people.

In my world, January slowly fades away in a haze of ice and snow, but I'm pretending things are coming up roses.

Yes, I'm still incredibly sore, possibly even more than I was this time a month ago. But then again, I do have a Ford F-150 to thank for that.

It was just enough of a blow to remind me I'm alive, and not merely living in a dream. Enough to wake me up to appreciate all the blessings I have.

My kids are so *loud*; they laugh, tease, love, torture, and fight with each other. One minute the best of friends, the next, bitter enemies.

As they should be.

And together, we'll navigate the minefields of friendship and family, returning always, inevitably, to this oasis of love.

The pendulum will continue to swing.

That's what pendulums do.

As sure as the weather, nothing lasts forever.

The -35 Celsius which greeted me last Tuesday has been replaced by a glorious -2 this morning.

My soul sings out at the reprieve as I begin the week, feeling more mellow yellow today, and a little less frozen and blue, even though they say it's the "bluest" day of the year.

## January 21st

### Still, life

I can remember a time
when we lived our lives
without stopping to capture them
when cameras were clunky
and photos took time
where you worried
something incriminating
may be seen by a stranger
behind the counter,
a flash you hadn't intended
now,
it's far too easy
a snapshot can travel
around the world and back
in the time it used to take
to drive to the store
is it progress
to take so many throw-away
still life images,
or are we forgetting how to live?
when each picture
is a millisecond,
lasting forever
how do we measure
the moments
between living and life?

## January 22nd

### Time slick

it's funny how time slides
an oil slick
sparkling
holographically
in the sun
until you turn
to take a glance
and look back
to find it gone
vanished
leaving only
a vague feeling
it was ever
there at all

## January 23rd

### The Forging

It's strange how routine invades,
making even the most bitter tastes
somehow okay again
it changes things,
smoothing them into the way
they've always been
I am a blade,
honed by hands wiser
in the forges of my destiny
each blow that lands
meant to strengthen
until finally,
I am dipped in the oil
where I could crack or harden
is that the moment
when you wonder
if you can go on?
the moment
where the universe pauses,
waiting for will-they
or won't-they?
but in the hands of the master
I emerge,
intact
glowing brilliant
in the red light of the hearth
able to take on the world
stronger than ever before

## January 24th

### Lucky Friday

another Friday
here at last
the weariness of the day
behind and long past
I drop off my bag,
change, and exhale
another long week
has passed, without fail
I hug my family
hold each of them tight
kiss my true love
and feel my soul take flight
home is where the heart is
or so it's been said
I smile at my good fortune
and head off to bed

## January 25th

### Burnout

Burnout is
not being able
to share your stress
because it will make people around you
feel worse
burnout is being a fixer
who can't fix,
trained to say yes
when saying no
is the right answer

## January 26th

It is always better
  to lighten one's burden
  by sharing the load
  instead of adjusting
  your backpack
  so it can hold more

## January 27th

Sudden death overtime  
cliff-hanger ends  
story interrupted  
my heart always rends  
I can’t wait to see  
what happens next  
I’m as captured by Sabrina  
as if I’ve been hexed

## January 28th

### Shackles of Society

We create
our own webs
of responsibility
choosing to wear them
like chokers,
and always heeling
to their demands
worry less about what others
may think
break free,
and lead a life of intention
instead of
a life of obligation

## January 29th

Angel number 2:34

So many days these three numbers are the first thing I see when I open my eyes.

Today, at 2:34 am, I once again rolled over to see the green glow of a digital clock to be greeted once more by the far too early yet familiar time.

So, on a whim, I looked it up and found out that when you keep seeing the same number in multiple places, it's called an angel number.

They are sent to catch our attention and tell us something important, or help us in some way with a problem we're having.

If the information I've found is correct, this particular number is telling me life is a roller coaster ride, one I need to be present to fully appreciate and enjoy while it lasts.

It wants me to know that the discoveries are never-ending, and I need to explore every bit of life to experience it completely.

It's interesting, because this number often greets me during periods of change.

Whether it's angels or anxiety, I can feel a tingle of excitement in the air, like ozone after a thunderstorm.

I can almost taste it on the breeze.

Change is always there, a short step behind the numbers.

As I roll over and close my eyes, not yet ready to wake up, I wonder which number will greet me tomorrow.

## January 30th

### On with the show

standing in a room
a thousand light bulbs await
one by one they brighten
their light blinding me
with its phosphorescent glow
when only a handful appear
the illumination is friendly
but will I survive
full exposure?
am I ready
to brave
such a clear world?
with trembling,
tentative steps
I stand on stage
chin held high,
I walk into my future

# CHAPTER THREE

# February 2020

## February 1st

### Homecoming

I woke with a jolt,
wondering who it was
who'd come to say goodbye
then I got the phone call
and I smiled
He'd finally gotten his wish
to be with her again
He'd outlived her
by longer than he'd hoped
despite his own frailty
and prayers
but yesterday night,
just as the month rolled over,
his sweetheart came to get him
hand in hand,

they climbed those gilded stairs,
going home together
for the last time

## February 2nd

### Destiny

Oceans crash
against the shore
driven by purpose
nothing more

### the moon exists

that's what she does
and cares not at all
for those who love

### The wind will blow

us back again
light and dark,
sun and rain

## February 3rd

A life worth living
the warmth of sun on my face,
turned toward the sky
sunrise in the morning,
so beautiful it makes me cry
the laughter of a child
so free and so true
storms rolling in
wind howling and blue
the crunch of snow
beneath my feet
smiling at a stranger
I happen to meet
long walks with good friends at my side
driving somewhere new
in a trusty old ride
so many moments
I can't list them all
none of them exciting
yet to me,
a siren's call
a moment of deep breathing
every now and then
helps me remember my why,
persist through adversity
and always,
always,
continue to try

## February 4th

### Meaning

What gives life meaning?

I've been reading the book, *On Being Mortal*, by Atul Gawande this week, and it's put me in a contemplative mood.

My thoughts run deeper than I like in my free time as I ponder on what allows us to continue moving forward despite the losses we incur. Sometimes those losses are subtle, and other times unbearably dramatic and cruel.

I've mulled it over and over, finding no good answers as I settle in to watch TV with my kids. And somehow, while introducing my kids to *Darkwing Duck*, I had a deep sense of knowing.

Sinking into the present,
into the *belonging*,
I allowed myself to feel
the cozy warmth of my youngest child, pressed tight against my left side,
hear the laughter of the older ones,
and smell the food cooking in the kitchen.
I was both intensely present in the now,
yet caught up in remembering.
Full circle.
My childhood combined with theirs,
and suddenly I'm five again.
This is how we do it.
These are the simple times that allow us to continue.

Meaning can be wherever we find it, whether in literature that has stood the test of time, a sweeping orchestral score, or even, sometimes, in cartoons and cuddles.

I'm so grateful I can find meaning with the ones I love, big and small, near and far.

Smiling at this unexpected epiphany in the everyday,
I sink further into the moment.

## February 5th

### House of Dreams

Silence descended
on this house of dreams
full of kids and kittens
love bursting
from the seams

## February 6th

### Purpose

Many things
are required to live
but only a few things
make life worth living

## February 7th

### No is a complete sentence

It's funny how
a simple no
can break the spell
wake you up
and let you see
how much you can do
for others
before it becomes
too much
but like a gust
from the Arctic
No
sweeps illusions away
making you realize
how easily
the word comes to others

## February 8th

### Five Questions

stuck in the mindset of how
without any solid reason why
I wonder what the heck I'm doing
and when things turned out this way
at least I know where I'm going
and who I'm going to be with
when I get there

## February 9th

### Sunday Night

another end and beginning
now the weekend is over,
and finally,
it's time for sleep
weariness surpasses my drive
as I sink into bed
the whooshing in my ears quiet for now
I wonder what the next week will bring
new adventures, challenges, gifts?
laughter and love,
or sadness and loss?
each day unique
even if the night offers
the same blanketing comfort
as darkness replaces day

## February 10th

### Monday Night Goofballs

I never knew it was possible to love someone so much. The way they drive you bonkers one minute, then melt your heart the next.

None of it seemed possible until I had my own children.

By turns sweet and vicious with each other, I cherish the times they are kind and share, and try hard to plug my ears when they shriek at each other over tiny transgressions.

Has it been almost nine years? It's hard to believe my little Alexis Rexis, Littlest Hobo, and Mattman are getting so big… and yet, they are.

We listen to them have nearly adult conversations in bewilderment, then laugh as we watch Darkwing Duck together and expand their minds. My little Monday night goofballs, getting so much bigger every day.

Don't they know they will always be my little ones?

## February 11th

### Growth Mindset

Embrace change,  
use it as an oar  
to power you to a new location  
learn from criticism,  
but don't be dragged down by negativity  
be inspired by others,  
not envious or defeated  
persist in the face of obstacles,  
but know when to cut your losses  
put in one hundred percent,  
but always know your limits  
and, above all else,  
accept your own humanity

## February 12th

### Bubbles

It's been awhile
since I last felt it,
that effervescent tingle
of bubbles
rising as fast
as helium in my heart
I smile and hug myself,
glorying in a ray of sunshine,
golden in happiness
as I turn my grateful face
to the sky

## February 13th

### Renewals

My heart broke today
watching as a couple exchanged vows
She was dressed in white,
ruffles on an ivory background
Wheeled to the front by her son
in a chrome and leather chariot,
her legs too frail
to hold her slight weight,
she wore the same dress she'd worn
when she'd first said I do
Back when love shone
in her now clouded and tired eyes.
His suit was black and neatly pressed,
a single red rose in the buttonhole
For a moment,
I saw a young man standing there,
fresh from the war,
about to marry his true love
His eyes twinkled,
as blue as ever,
as he stared at her with joy
once again,
he spoke those words wholeheartedly
The years may have robbed her
of the memory of their vows,
but his remained strong
as he once again promised
to love, honour, and cherish her,

in sickness and health,
til death do us part
For better or worse

## February 14th

### Love

Sunrise brings me
rose-coloured glasses
I love you as much
as ginger snaps
love molasses

## February 15th

### Mountain Mornings

I love the quiet
of the almost-dawn
the crunch of snow
beneath my feet
the stars twinkle
while the earth
holds her breath,
waiting for the sun
to enter from the east
and wake her from
her long night of rest

## February 16th

### Banff

Jagged peaks
now softened by snow
the sun shines
the winter winds blow
I love your majesty
and all of your might
but most of all
I love you at night

## February 17th

### Undone

it's hiding in plain sight,
right on the tip of my tongue
what is it I'm forgetting?
what have I left undone?
is it an assignment…
no, that's not it
maybe it's the housework?
nah, that doesn't fit
so, what is it I've shirked?
I look at my list, my phone
and even my kid
but it's not an easy answer—
could it be my Id?
it *has* been forever
since I've paid it any heed
whenever I'm awake I'm busy,
so maybe that's what I need
I'll take a little fun time,
and greet my oldest friend
and then, perhaps,
this feeling will finally end

## February 18th

### Anticipation of Elation

I spent the first hour of my morning scrolling, finding it hard to motivate myself to do anything else. I'm not sure why. There's plenty for me to do. Maybe my brain just needs a break.

I'm starting to feel like I'm smack dab in the middle of a huge life event. Like something big is looming, or like I'm eight, and the week before Christmas is finally here.

Anticipation is KILLING me.

But nothing is happening—yet.

Is it work? Home? Writing? An exciting trip I haven't yet planned? What fabulous event is waiting for me, just over the horizon? (I'm hoping it's something good coming. Let me dream, okay?)

For now, until I figure it out, I'll pick myself up from indecision and focus on my never ending to-do list.

Just like a kid eating veggies to get to my dessert.

I think I can, I think I can.

## February 19th

### Strength

when clouds surround you
and wind gusts knock you down
when you're sure
you can't take any more
at the end of your rope
is where you'll find purpose
and the strength
to carry on

## February 20th

Change for coffee?
expectation
and anticipation
of change is here
simmering like dark roast
in my veins
with a tantalizing,
full-bodied aroma
making the wait
well worth the pain

## February 21st

### Winds of Change

can knock you down
take away your breath
and leave you wondering
what happened
but despite the ferocity,
despite the pain,
freedom emerges
from the ashes,
begins a new life
transformed
a fresh inferno will rise
standing tall
without the fetters
that held me down
I will spread my wings
and fly free

## February 22nd

### Saturday night, after the bomb

It's hard to express the level of my dismay.

Imagine studying for twelve years. Missing out on much of your twenties, moving away from home several times to become something you'd been dreaming of since you were little.

Helping, being there. Wanting to change the world.

Then slowly, the world changes, but not how you expected it to. Suddenly, people begin to make you feel bad about earning money, even though it took a full ten years to pay back the cost of the education you had to borrow from the bank.

Even though some days turn into three, or a week. Even a month, once, before kids and that was possible.

The longest I ever worked was 32 days in a row, half of which were 24 hour shifts. Many of which involved no sleep.

Because I was needed.

I was making a difference.

Money is nice, but it isn't why anyone does it.

In fact, it's usually another ten or twenty years of insane hours of work before you can call yourself out of debt from your training after the training is done.

I look to social media, and see millionaires everywhere, smiling and shiny, influencing other people, often without any qualifications. Listened to, admired.

Compared to me, and I'm found wanting, less trustworthy than a movie/porn star giving medical advice. What they are now calling "the death of expertise".

And my single employer (because we have no other option) tells me they are cutting my income by 36$/hr. Which would be fine, if my expenses were covered, but out of what I have left, I have to pay to run my own business, whose costs haven't decreased.

Leaving me with a negative cash inflow at the end of a work day. Less take home pay than I've had since I worked retail when I was a teen.

For minimum wage.

Because I'm lazy, wasteful, or both.

Clearly I am wasteful, but I know I'm not lazy.

It's hard not to wonder why I wasted so much time training for something no one seems to think worth the cost. Decades where I could have had vacations and enjoyed my family, not to mention maybe having a few savings in the bank instead of so much debt.

And then, to make matters worse, we are told "you don't understand," and that, "it wouldn't be sensible," to leave.

Oh, and sign a contract for this other plan which you don't qualify for.

True Story.

Except sensible left the building months ago.

When people without medical backgrounds decide what should and should not be paid for in our healthcare system, everyone suffers.

I don't understand why knowledge has no value today. Why everyone but me understands what my patients need. No one asked us, the people doing the work.

It's like me telling a teacher how to teach, or a lawyer how to address a jury.

Or my dad how to fix my car.

It just doesn't make sense, and it doesn't end up working out in the long run.

But I'm not defeated yet.

I still have time to put value where I want to. And if my employer is going to treat me like garbage, I'll do what I've done in the past.

First, I'll try to change my situation by standing up.

By using the voice God gave me to shout it to the rooftops.

And if no one will listen, which has happened before, and will likely happen again, then I will chart a new course.

## February 23rd

### Vigilance

2:16

Again, I wonder, why this time of day? Too early to wake up, too late to successfully fall asleep once more.

Is it the soft snores of my little one, or the louder sawing emanating from my husband?

Perhaps it's the sound of my conscience screaming, telling me it's time, there's much work to be done, people to protect.

I will stand up for those who cannot rise, raise my voice for those who've lost their own.

All it takes for bad men to succeed is for good people to stand by watching, and that has never been my way.

For some reason, I prefer the uphill climb.

The summit is much sweeter when earned.

And oh, they shall hear me coming.

I will be strong, and I will be standing with others who refuse to remain silent in the face of great wrongs.

Like the trees standing by the river, we shall not be moved.

On ne bouge pas.

## February 24th

### Decision

all my motivation has left,
I've nothing more to do
my give-a-damn is busted
and it's all because of you
when you work until your fingers break
and get told it's not enough,
tossed upon the scrap heap—
man, it makes life rough
so much for trying,
so much for give and take,
now I have to figure out
if my purpose is worth the ache

## February 26th

### Bedtime

moments of comfort
glimpses
of joy
wrapped up
tight
with my girls
and my boy

## February 28th

The last day of the shortest month of the year, but it has felt so long.

I'm tired. Épuisé.

I wrack my brain, certain I've been here before, but I'm too tired to remember. Packed in bubble wrap, I'm numb.

I sit in silence, unable to create, and idly wonder where my spark has gone. Maybe if I could sleep, like Aurora did for a hundred years.

But I've never been a princess, too constrained by such a mold.

It's my lot in this life to be the loud one.

To speak out, wear my heart on my sleeve, and stand up in front. Protect those who can't protect themselves, despite the cost.

Maybe this time, I'll finally earn some rest.

CHAPTER FOUR

# March 2020

## March 1st

Spring Change

Spring and change walk hand in hand
bringing new life,
new air,
new purpose
I turn my chin toward the sun,
close my eyes and breathe the fresh, cool air
change waits for no one
Spring's work has once again begun

## March 2nd

A Hard Monday morning

I'm halfway through my first cup of coffee when he comes looking for me.

His plaintive voice cries out a title only three can use without irony, and soon, the cats amplify the call.

Silence has vanished, and now he's crying in earnest because his nose is stuffy. It's dry in here and it's been bothering him for days, but of course, he won't let me help him blow it.

In vain, I try to get him to stop hitting himself as he swipes wildly at it, but he's still half asleep, angry at how his face has failed him.

Yes, dear, I agree. Mondays are hard.

Then, before I can do or say anything else, he's asleep again, curled up beside me with the cats.

Snoring.

## March 3rd

### Morning Reflections

I love the still
of the early morning
now that life
is a never ending rush
toward the night
Dawn gives a chance
to pause,
reflect,
and appreciate
everything that's bright

## March 4th

### Brain Bugs

busy brain,
please let me sleep
in my bed
nice and deep
you run along
a mile a minute
even though I beg
you remain obstinate
things to do
stories to see,
and so I sigh,
grateful
for my coffee

## March 5th

Another day closer
to something
I can't see
the only question left
is whether I've gone
past halfway
or have already reached
my goal

## March 6th

### Dinosaur Dreaming

Woolly Mammoths
Albertasaurus Rex,
with my troop of brownies
we took a little trek
to a dinosaur museum
where we'd spend the night
sleeping under triceratops
while the moon was bright
and in the silent darkness
the skeletons came alive
Mesozoic and Cenozene
they all walked and thrived
in the land before time
it was like nothing I'd ever seen
but in the morning they were silent again—
like last night had never been

## March 7th

### Family time

safe
in my home
loved ones
tucked in tight
I'm happy to watch
an old movie
cuddle up,
and turn out the light

## March 8th

### Sunday

full of plans
the week arrives
hat in hand
looking sheepish
just because
once again
they forgot
to pause

## March 9th

### Seashells

my wheels spin,
trying to gain traction
on the sands of time
so many things left to do
with the day just beginning
I've taught my children
to count to ten
and breathe
shouldn't I know how
to do it too?
yet somehow it's harder
in this social media world
closing my eyes,
I try again
and hear the ocean crash
inside my mind

## March $10^{th}$

Sleeping cats
sleek and warm
curled up like
eiderdown
fluffy soft coats
black and striped with brown
as they purr and meow
they remind me to live
and appreciate being
in the here and now

## March 11th

### Pandemic

an eerie mood
has gripped the world
like the calm
in the eye of the storm
the hair on my neck
prickles
as I think of Stephen King
then sighing,
I shake my head
and wash my hands
again

## March 12th

Epuisé
the sand from the day
blankets my eyes
fatigue
falls to the side
finding comfort
in the arms of Morpheus
and with him,
finally,
I descend

## March $13^{th}$

### Friday the 13th

I find myself thinking
of the Knights of the Order of St. John.
Whether at one point truly noble,
or the devils they were persecuted for being,
the Order fought for king and country
until the day they burned for their sins.
Now, I feel the change on the wind.
Donning my own armour of gloves,
mask, and gown, stethoscope—
freshly wiped down—
and my scrubs to keep me calm,
I enter the fray.
I'll do my best to protect the innocent,
not knowing if the inquisition awaits me, too,
once this battle is done.

## March 14th

The count went up by ten today.

My heart lurched as nausea set in. Yesterday was four, the day before, I don't remember.

But, *ten*.

The number hit me hard.

It's time to hunker down, work on reflection, and all those projects I've said I'd get to one day.

Time to be the homebody again, like when my newborns were fresh. The days ran together then, each one the same, but no less precious. Little heartbeats close to mine, the promise of the future so bright.

Even as fear grips me with its sharpness, my little one curls up beside me and, holding my hand, falls asleep.

## March 15th

In my cozy nest
we got the news I'd been expecting.
schools cancelled,
lives upended
I gather my loved ones close,
thankful I can continue to work
sad for those who have to choose
have there ever been more painful words
than "for the greater good"?

## March 16th

### Insult to Injury

why do you kill the morale
of those about to fight?
why do you want to hurt them?
is it solely out of spite?
when everything is confusing
and spins out of control
heaping insult on injury
leaves society with a heavy toll
one that will resound for years
long after this illness has past
people who will regret
that they received
exactly what they asked

## March 17th

A day for Revelry and Parades
now shut down and silent
faces taut,
afraid
as I pass them in the store
shelves empty in odd ways
no canned fruit,
but plenty of vegetables
the toilet paper aisle is empty,
but an abundance of Tide
people standing arms distance away
as they wait for the Self-check stands
furtive looks right and left,
then out into the cold again
safe in my nest,
I rinse and dress for bed
ready to repeat it all again

## March 18th

### The Blanket

It won't be done on time.

I've already accepted my dreams outpace my ability to achieve them. I plan things without any sense of time, focusing instead on the goal.

The shiny gold ring at the end.

I wanted it to be a present for my husband's birthday, two weeks from now, but life, as they say, is what happens when you're making other plans.

The last few weeks have been a blur of indecision, uncertainty, and pain. But now, as I accept my shortcomings, I'm soothed by the simple task at hand.

Single crochet, single, double crochet, repeat.

Like the sound of my breathing, it continues rhythmically despite my turmoil.

Repeat, repeat, repeat.

## March 19th

### The Eternal Tide

waves crash against the shore
spraying me with the salt
of a thousand years
the brine of tears cried
by loved ones lost
centuries distant
from where I now stand
closing my eyes,
I hear the echo of voices,
reminding me
we are all part of the whole
together we rise and ebb
waves in the ocean,
brushing against the beach
in life's eternal tide

## March 20th

### Truth

You can live alone,
or surrounded by others
but only when you remain
true to your values
unswayed
by the winds around you
will you ever feel at home

## March 21st

### Spring

and then it was time
somehow,
Winter passed
the days ran away
as Spring snuck in
at last
sun warmed the ground,
pushed the snow aside
I smile and face the mountains
listening
as my children play outside

## March 22nd

### Spring Run

My head is buzzing
from the sunshine,
as time,
golden and fleet of foot
slides through my fingers,
brushing past the tips
before it trickles away
deceptively plentiful
until I turn
and miss it once again
I close my eyes,
and allow my legs
to find their way

## March 23rd

### Change on the Horizon

an inner restlessness is growing,
a need to see something new
stretch beyond my boundaries,
stop staring into the wild blue
in a little while I'll be ready
to travel past my own backyard
as soon as I take the first step,
the rest won't be as hard

## March 24th

### Facing Mortality

This month has left me stunned
and in awe of those around me
I see people coping
through it all
and I wonder
how much of our mental health struggles
come from a lack of purpose
or clarity
on why we want to live
perhaps in order
to truly feel alive in a moment
we need to face
the possibility of death

## March 25th

### PB&J haiku

rocking a sandwich,
peanut butter and jelly
mini eggs and smiles

## March 26th

**Perpetual motion machine**

watching my five year old Namaste,
I'm struck by the way
he's in motion
even when sitting still
where did my energy go?
when did it disappear
into the mist?
was it when I put my nose
to the grindstone
or after,
when I gave my life for his?
or was it when I forgot
how to be a child
and see the world
for how amazing
it really is?

## March 27th

TWENTY POUND WEIGHTS
pull my eyelids to ground
tomorrow is another mountain
but I won't let it get me down
there's a present waiting,
over on the other side
it makes the effort worth it—
remembering the climb
is more than worth the ride

## March 28th

### Perseverance

Some roads are dark
others hidden
and strange
but there's always light
where you least expect it
if only
you allow it in

## March 29th

### Gaslight

in the midst of the storm,
we feel defeated and demoralized
told we have to
because no one can replace us,
while simultaneously that anyone
can do what we do,
that we don't deserve to be so lucky
to earn what we do,
to be valued for our calling
we struggle through because
we believe
all life has value
but each blow that falls
dents our paper masks a little more
I kiss my children's heads as I tuck them in
wondering when I'll be forced to choose
between my family
and my vocation

## March 30th

### Pandora's Box

I feel the heaviness around me
but it's tinged
with odd excitement
change is here,
and it's hard
yet, trailing along,
like a best friend forgotten
is the whisper of hope
Pandora opened her box,
and the plague descended
but the answer is close behind
the bad we see is
just the tide washing up
on the beach
and soon,
it will subside
because Hope
is on the way

## March 31st

The end of another month,
just me and my quarterly review
I'm left wondering again
how it so quickly flew
my loved one's anniversary—
I thank heaven for him
soon it will be spring
nature's annual whim
with tomorrow only for fools
I wonder who it will be—
will it be the government
or, will it instead
be me?

CHAPTER FIVE

# April 2020

pril 1st

Mantra for 2020

free my heart from hate,
my mind from worry,
my soul from shame

## April 2nd

### The Winner

built Ford tough
taking the hits
like I'm in the ring
made out of rubber
I keep bouncing back
tougher,
wiser,
knowing at the end
it's not who wins or loses
but the one still standing
integrity
and heart intact
who wins the prize

## April 3rd

### Tightrope Walker

waiting
without wilting,
chin up,
but not too far
being calm
without looking cold,
remaining who you are
each day is a tightrope
each step
could be your last
but when you reach
the other side
you can look back,
and laugh

## April 4th

### What I Know For Sure

I can't control the weather
but my mind is only mine
I can't control those around me
but I'm in charge of all my time
maybe I can't change the world
but I can grow and stretch
I'm in control of something
no one else can ever catch
I may not go down in history
but that's okay, you see
because at the end of the day
I'm always proud of me

## April 5th

### Sunday Thoughts

Another weekend has come and gone
and I'm grateful for my blessings
in the midst of upheaval,
and news that gets worse by the day,
I'm surrounded by love
in my castle,
with my family,
and we have everything we need
it's not fancy,
but it's everything I've ever wanted
as the weekend slinks in,
I close my eyes
and give thanks

## April 6th

### Nature simply IS

It's Monday, week three of our self-imposed exile.

I've been up since 2:30, wide awake and not sure why.

The best I can determine is that nine hours of sleep on a luxurious weekend of nothing impacted how much sleep debt I had, thus rendering my alarm unnecessary, but coffee more useful than usual by 6:30.

As I watched the sun rise, I was reminded once more that fairness is a concept nature abhors.

Life is life, simple and complete, perfect as it unfolds, no matter if we planned for it to be something different.

Yawning, I savour the moment, inhaling my bitter brew as I look into the future once more.

## April 7th

### Why

The reason why
I do what I do
is simple
for my babies,
my raison d'être(s)
I will be the example
of everything they deserve
to be and have
in this world
love,
hard work,
compassion,
and most of all,
gratitude and joy

## April 8th

### Earth

brewing clouds
lift the gauze
of life beneath
our human laws
we see the truth
for what it's worth
we must understand
we share this earth

## April 9th

### Now is the Time

slowing down
hasn't happened yet
I'm left wondering
what it is
I did forget
in spite of the extra time
or perhaps, it's because of
I'm spinning my wheels
doing nothing of what I love
it's time to make a break,
finish with the old
but first,
build my courage—
for now is a time to be bold

## April 10th

### Good Friday

What's so good about the day
we sacrificed the divine among us?
As I drive to work,
I wonder how is the sacrifice of one
to save the many entwined so tightly
with our humanity
as far back as stories,
mothers and fathers, children,
even strangers have died for others
We each have the potential,
and once activated,
we are transcendent
no longer merely human
we become sacrificial lambs
nature is full of this same conundrum—
lemmings, wasps, the faithful pet
will give their all for the many
we are all part of nature;
we all come from the divine

## April 11th

### Saturday Vibes

It's the pause
between death
and rebirth
while inside
there's a hush
the world continues on
sunrise, sunset
winds blow,
tides roll in and out
but we are
forever changed

## April 12th

### Easter Sunday

Reading the alchemist
looking at the morning stars
I'm filled with peace
as the universe pauses,
exhales
we are all on a journey
the world has a soul
did God create the desert
for us to appreciate the oasis?
what we put out into the world
we receive back in full
even the sun and the wind
bow to the hand
that created the soul
of the world

## April 13th

### Easter Monday

we rise again
on Easter Monday
following the light
from our creator above
and here on earth
the sun still shines
hearts refill
once more
with love

## April 14th

### Mine

that's how I think of them
all mine to care for,
protect,
keep safe if possible
I know it's not up to me—
it never is in the end
it's always heartbreaking
when reality intrudes
and nature takes over,
when we have
to say goodbye

## April 15th

### An Affable Chap

easy going,  
but ready to leave  
together  
we coaxed him to stay  
with memories of childhood  
and a spot of tea  
watching fat snowflakes  
cover the naked trees

## April 17th

### Mulan and my children

Watching Mulan with my kids,
I'm reminded what it means to be a woman
Now, and then
No one can stop me from living my life
just because I was born female
A history lesson ensued
and my children learned how recently women
achieved the right to vote,
to be doctors,
police officers,
politicians
I watched them sit straighter,
and set their chins high
I smiled, knowing with pride
No one will tell my children they can't
just because they were born a certain way
if Mulan could save China,
when she was supposed to stay at home

## April 18th

### George's Nest

my bed is cozy,
feathered and light
made with scraps of fabric,
sparkling
and bright
I turn in circles,
before snuggling in
I'm Bengal on my dad's side
I think with a grin

## April 19th

### A Mother Lost

Sunday was productive,
a day of sunshine and smiles
until I saw the news
one dark heart,
twisted by life's challenges
took the sun away from others
replacing joy
with unimaginable grief
while my children shriek with glee,
she'll never see hers again

## April 20th

Is today 4/20?
I forget
too busy
surviving Monday
in a time of regret

## April 21st

### My Boys

two boys so different,
yet still the same
babies of the family,
with nougat centres,
but a tough-guy shell
they set their chin just so—
and no one can ever tell

## April 22nd

### Gratitude

grateful for the sun
on my face
the slap of my feet
on the sidewalk
the morning breeze
cools me
the sky a clear
and brilliant blue
the peaks of the mountains,
white and jagged
cut the sky in two

## April 23rd

### Allergies and Frisky-bits

“the frisky-bit hit the tree with the pussy willows,
and the dust made my eyes itchy
and then the sky cried and it was fine
and oh yeah—I have super-strength-cat power!”
such a vibrant world they live in,
I wish I could stay with them awhile
the colours are brighter there,
the powers more exciting,
inside the creative mind of a child

## APRIL 24TH

### ADVICE TO MYSELF

we are so accustomed
to doing what "is right"
we push our needs aside—
as women,
as daughters,
as mothers
but at the end of the day,
you are the only one
who can decide
what is right for you

## April 26th

### Butterflies of Indecision

scattered
the butterflies tickle
up by my throat
trying to break free
into the sun
where freedom waits
but,
unable to choose a direction
they swirl,
swirl,
swirl,
looking for the light

## April 27th

### Aunty's Birthday

ear to ear grins
kisses from chubby hands
sun shining brightly
we bring birthday cheer
while the youngest
steals the show again

## April 28th

### Almost Birthday Musings

has it been almost a year
since my last revolution
around the sun?
since I made a list
and vowed the next year
would be "the one"?
where I'd appreciate
all life had to offer
in some ways I've done better,
in others, not so much
but I'm here again
smiling at the idea
this year— this one—
will finally be the one
and I'll get it right at last

## April 29th

### We will remember

What will we remember,
once this time has past?
Days of endless nothing?
Or the quiet that fell at last?

Will we remember how much
we desperately missed each other
how much we missed our friends,
our mom, dad, sisters, and brothers?

Will it be the lack of travel
and the new horizons we'll miss the most?
I wonder what will we marvel at
when this bug finally gives up the ghost.

CHAPTER SIX

# May 2020

## May 1st

Gus

what a cute surprise
a May Day puppy
with soft brown eyes
fit for wooing
any family

## May 2nd

Spring is here

So many things are changing
yet spring enters
anyway
unstoppable,
unbothered by the fuss
she returns
whether we're deserving
or not
on her own schedule,
bringing soft breezes
and the laughter of birds
frolicking in dawn's early blush
afternoon lingers into the night
and we fall sleep on the promise
her inconstancy will be there
forever

## May 3rd

### Unsettled

during a time of unrest
storm clouds cover the sky above
I close my eyes and focus
on the sounds of thunder

## May 4th

### May Rains

rain speckles my glasses
leaves tingles on my skin
so fresh
the earth
drinks it in
rivulets of silver
after the ice of winter
retreats

## May 5th

### Belong

what's in a patch of dirt
that lets you call it home?
what makes one belong
no matter where they roam?
it's in the way you feel
deep inside your soul—
you can fit most anywhere
when your heart is whole

## May 6th

### Dreams

they run through my sleep
friends from my youth
last glimpsed
decades ago
they wave
and we embrace
catching up on
a youth well spent
leaving me with a smile
when I open my eyes
in a time when we are far apart
isn't it nice
we can be forever close
in heart?

## May 7th

### Leap of faith

last night I dreamed
I was on a rocky ledge
cracks appeared
but just in time,
I leapt to safer ground
I knew instantly
now was the moment
to take a leap of faith
and on waking
was ready at last
to face the world

## May 8th

### Someone

there's always someone
who makes you shine,
builds you up,
thinks you hung the moon
someone loves you
just the way you are
misses you
when you're gone
and thinks of you
night and day

## May 9th

### How to cook Chili—as told by a mom, doing her best.

Today I made Chili.

I had to get the hamburger out of the freezer and defrost it. I collected all the ingredients, finding one lonely pepper and a bunch of celery, which I cut while making macaroni for the kids lunch.

I accidentally opened tomato paste instead of stewed tomatoes, which reminded me the kids were out of cheese pizza.

I was pretty sure I had the ingredients for that as well, so I made bread dough, then felt I should make cinnamon buns too.

Somehow in the process, I also did a few loads of laundry when I couldn't find towels to mop up the inevitable mess.

I spent the day going from one room to the next in a perpetual cycle of reminders and wondering, "Why did I come in here again?"

And in the end, I froze the chili for later (even though it was supposed to be for supper) and we ate pizza and cinnamon buns with happy kids while watching a movie.

And it was all because I tried to make a nice, simple chili for supper.

## May 10th

### Mother's Day

pure iron
in a satin coating
how else
could anyone
wake up every night
to feed their young,
wipe their tears,
and one day
somehow
let them go?

## May 11th

### Spring Snow Falling

It's May and it's snowing
I'm taken back to my birthday
was I seven,
or was I eight?
wearing my favourite play set,
shivering as a sunny day turned icy,
a cold front sweeping in
a spring blizzard
such an adventure for a kid!
now,
I wrap myself up tight in blankets
longing for bed,
and for the summer sun
to visit me once again

## May 12th

### Insomnia

so many sleepless nights
in adulthood
I envy my youth
when the bed
was always soft
and I could close my eyes,
lucid dreaming
until the daylight found me
now,
I stare at the ceiling
willing my brain
to shush it's mouth
and dread how early
the next day will arrive

## May 13th

### The Night Before

another year turns its back
I consider everything
come and gone
I flip another page
thinking of the days ahead
and those long past
vowing (again)
to make the most
of the future,
and give the past it's due
and above of all else,
keep striving to become
the best me
I'm meant to be

## May 14th

### Birthday Cake Blues

full of cake and buttercream,
I find my attempts to plan ahead
more challenging than ever
not knowing which direction to go
should I use this upheaval as a chance
to chart a new course,
second star to the right,
and straight on til morn?
or should I hold fast
until life settles down?
regardless of what next year holds
I'll hold my loved ones close
and today, full of cake,
I'll retire for the night
content in the knowledge
I'm where I'm supposed to be
and for this moment,
the future can take care of itself

## May 15th

### The Day After (my birthday)

cruising into the long weekend
once again I'm tricked
into thinking I have more time
than I really do
I'm certain I'll blink
and find it's Monday
but for now,
I bask in the extra freedom

## May 16th

### Sunny Saturday

sunshine brightens my day
while my kids dance and play
pretending to be Waterboy and Icegirl,
the silent puppy
waiting by the gate
as their imaginations run wild
the puppy bolts
shrieks erupt
as the fifteen pound pup
transforms into the monster
in their game
finally catching up with them
they tumble into a heap
of giggles and licks

## May 18th

### Puppy Dreams

deep sighs
he stretches out
our furry little baby,
taking a nap
on a warm spring day

## May 19th

Today

I will achieve
even if powered
only by caffeine
and my dreams

## May 20th

### Rainy Day

Wednesday morning
waterfalls
rustling in the dark
the sounds of nature
waking up
leaves a special mark

## May 21st

### Goal setting and reality checks

I'm in the midlife crisis years— at least, the timing works out.

If the average age life expectancy for a woman is somewhere into the mid-eighties, then here I am. Guilty!

I don't know how much of my current state of restlessness is from my age, or due to our current social distancing rules.

Covid 19 has altered society in unanticipated ways.

"We're all in this together even though we're far apart"

#togetherathome

#social distancing

##### ad infinitum.

Blah.

If I'm being honest, this feeling has been brewing for a while. Possibly since before having children, but definitely since they've been on the scene.

There's so many things in life I still want to do. I know I've achieved more of my dreams than most people do, but I'm still searching for answers, feeling there's something more I need to know, do, become, experience.

I've listened to Michelle Obama's book, and it resonated with me in many ways. It was the first time I'd ever considered a woman so respected and admired around the world, from a different country, upbringing, and lifestyle, is someone I could be friends with.

Perhaps it's just the magic of reading a really good book. I'm sure the audiobook helped, read in her own voice as it was, but it was more than that.

I felt a heart-deep connection.

Her life has been so varied and, while I'd never wish for half the stress she experienced before or after entering the world's spotlight, it made me reexamine what I have become.

What I would *still* like to become.

I read it just as coronavirus entered into our world and our lives changed forever.

I watched, horrified, when China built a hospital in a week.

That was the moment I knew we were in for something terrible in 2020, but I had no idea of the scale.

Coming into the new year, my mantra was "Seeing clearly in 2020", but it's harder to do now than it's ever been.

How can I prepare or plan when I don't know what the world will be in one month from now, let alone one or five years from now?

But over the last two months, dealing with the anxiety and fear and overwhelm, the loss of those both close and unknown, I was reminded of one simple fact.

None of us have ever known what would happen in a month or year. We've gone about our days as if we did, making plans for that mythical "what if and someday", but inevitably, life happens without checking our wish lists.

So yes, I do plan on seeing clearly in 2020.

But maybe the clearest part is understanding and accepting my own lack of control. I can plan and wish and dream, but at the end of the day, life will happen, regardless of what I tell it to do.

So maybe my new goal will be accepting that.

I'll try— but, I am only human after all.

## May 22nd

### Face Off

eyes narrowed
they face each other
her hackles up,
she's unimpressed,
his ears perked,
the puppy waits
for his moment

## May 23rd

### Pandemic Birthday Party

Today we made movie magic
at home
tickets printed,
party crowns made
they've talked of nothing else
all week
excited beyond belief
a special birthday party
for a family of five
to celebrate
a special child

## May 24th

### Spring Sunday

another Sunday
drifting away
pussy willows
become shoots of green
a saucy robin taunts me
while a spring breeze
tickles my skin
impossibly soft
I walk on wet streets
left behind
by ice retreating
watching winter's grip
finally release

## May 25th

### The Edge of the Unknown

standing on the brink
of what's known
and yet to come
there lies a gulf
where monsters
and angels lurk
ready to leap
grabbing the ankle
of the unwary

## May 26th

### Feelings

emotions are waves
that can pull you down
and sweep you away
if you allow them
half a chance

## May 27th

### Loudest Silence

a new place
a brand new bed
strange silence looms
the noise grows louder
unchecked
alone
in my head

## May 28th

### Walk into the wildness

I took a walk
in the wilderness
turned my face to the sun
lilacs bloomed around me
a moment stretched
into eternity

## May 29th

### The Longest Shower

I showered today
as long as I wanted
with no one yelling
at me through the door
luxuriating in the stream
of near-scalding water
it felt like forever
but when I looked at the clock
only fifteen minutes had passed

## May 30th

### Change

a change is as good as a rest
at least, so my father has often said
from the time a person is little
right up until they're dead
I think that he was right
at least for me, the story is true
because the only thing I've regretted
is staying stuck and feeling blue

## May 31st

### Last day

one more deep breath
of this purple
lilac-scented air
time-out-of-time
blink;
and it's gone

CHAPTER SEVEN

# June 2020

J une 1st

HOMECOMING

anticipation of return added wings to my feet
but held down by gravity,
time dragged on
until finally, bags dropped to the floor,
aching arms were filled
by soft hugs from freshly bathed children
and at last—my heart is home

## June 2nd

### Home day

a day spent at home with children
catch up as catch can
planning a week already half done
while we wait for dad to return

## June 3rd

### Rush

back to the daily grind
turn another page
take a deep breath
close your eyes
time passes
like fireflies in a storm

## June 4th

### Three

Has it already been three months
since our lives changed,
since the world
was forced to stop
and hold its breath
three months
since the dolphins
returned to the canals
and deer began to roam
city streets
the earth has a fever
but as the skies become more blue
I wonder if the cure is worse
than the disease
of me and you

## June 5th

### Forgotten

The overwhelming sensation
of something left undone
I've forgotten something
or maybe,
it's someone?
the list of what I have to do
grows longer by the day
and while I sit and wonder
time just slips away

## June 6th

### A Good Day

full of hard work
the reward lies in the doing
and accomplishment
is merely delicious icing
on the cake

## June 7th

### Change

change is inevitable
but does it arrive
on the winds of the summer
or buzzing of bees from a hive?
will it whisper sweet nothings,
like a lover in the dark
or does it leave something behind
a tangible, permanent mark?
it's hard to pin down
but one thing I know is true
you never need to go looking
because change will always find you

## June 8th

### Monday Vibes

a Monday roll-by
sleepy
rainy
low pressure sighs
the lion lays down
with the wolf
cozy
on the couch

## June 9th

### Organizing

there is something
so soothing
about stationary
and making plans
never mind
they gang aft agley
more often than not

## June 10th

### Promises

*"You'll be my mom even when you die, and then you'll be waiting for me in heaven."*

Words of wisdom
over nachos and cheese
hurting my heart with love
the way only
a five-year-old can

## June 11th

### Early Mornings

the sounds of the city
not yet begun
me,
alone
face turned
toward
the rising sun

## June 12th

### Rainy Night

A deluge
outside my door,
rain pounding
to get in
I curl up
in the blankets,
falling asleep
with a grin

## June 13th

### My Backyard

Fresh,
gently washed
by the rain
then air dried
with care
green grass pops,
pussy willows flutter
this city backyard
is a paradise

## June 14th

### A Rain Washed Day

Sunday morning
freshly cleaned
torrents of rain
wiping the dust
of winter away
leaving sparkling life
glowing in its wake

## June 15th

### My Choices

dreaming of a day
when all the work is done
nothing left to say
and time to have some fun
then I realize
tomorrow never comes
if I want music
in my life
I can't settle
just for hums

## June 16th

### Monday Hour One

so many ideas
so much I want to do
spinning, spinning, spinning
I must choose a path
because not choosing
is a choice too
do I commit,
or
do I allow my dreams
to drift with the clouds,
waiting for the wind
to guide my way?

## June 17th

### The Answers Within

silence grows my thoughts
boils them 'til they scream
showing me that life
is only how big I dream
I catch glimpses of the future,
the wonders that could be
I know if I look harder
the true magic lies in me

## June 18th

### Counting Seconds

a few hours of freedom—
what to do,
what to do?
it feels like
juicy goodness,
but far too easy
to burn through!

## June 19th

### The Age of Aquarius

the time of philosophers is here again
Pluto collides with Mercury,
ushering in the age of Aquarius
in a rocky delivery
belonging to the old world
is no longer good enough
we all must walk new roads
experience strange ideas.
fear will bow to love,
the only achievements of value
will be knowing yourself
and kindness to your neighbour
the earth will heal,
providing a place for everything
and everything a new place
nothing lacks when we stand together
brave enough to strive and fail
all equal at last

## June 20th

### Summer Solstice

I watched the sun
climb over the henge
saw the writing
on the rocks
breathing deep,
I heard the ages speak
comforting me
with their permanence

## June 21th

### Father's Day

John Denver plays the soundtrack
every year on Father's Day
I think of how blessed I've been
by the men in my life
their wisdom, strength, and kindness
one taught me to stand up and fight
now I watch as another
teaches our children the same
gifts beyond measure,
gratitude beyond words

## June 22nd

### Another Monday

fresh with possibilities
I wake with the dawn
to chase them
little fireflies
in the sky
glorious in their array
and always
only
one leap away

## June 23rd

### After Coffee Goals

creaky before my coffee
I let magic beans
elevate my mind
once my body
catches up
I'll find new mountains
I will climb

## June 24th

### Postcards from the Past

every day I write
I send a postcard
from my past
this time may be gone
but on the page
my memories
will live on

## June 25th

### What if

what if it was possible
to understand another
the way we know ourselves?
would we be more loving
if we spoke the same tongue
or would we still see
their face as other
when we look into their eyes?

## June 26th

HOW DO YOU STAND
and continue to fight
against a machine
that's strayed from what's right?
do you bow down,
and surrender your will
knowing full well
they mean nothing but ill?
or do you rage, rage
against the dying of the light
and never back down
and as you enter into night?

## June 27th

### Edge of Summer

every year,
my mind goes back
end of school,
my little brother's birthday
the days all run together now
but sometimes,
I still get to pause
and turn my face
toward the sun

## June 28th

### Dream Cottage

I'd love to have a writing shed—
a place to hide away
I'd put it by the tomato bed
and have a spell to say
so that no one else
could find me there
unless I let them in
it's a place I wouldn't share
my little book writing
cozy-office-masterpiece,
oh, how I'd while away the hours
my ideas would never cease!
regardless of achievement though,
I'd still like a hide-y-hole
to sit and let my writing out
and feed my creative soul

## June 29th

### Daydreaming

early mornings
are my favourite
when the air is
fresh and clean
I curl up
in a blanket
and let myself
daydream

## June 30th

### Breaking Free

the old restlessness is back,
so it's time to hit the road,
head out on the highway
release that heavy daily load
with sunshine comes adventure—
at least, that's what I hope
better than the usual drudgery
no time to sit around and mope

CHAPTER EIGHT

# July 2020

## JULY 1ST

CANADA DAY
on soil that was taken away
from nature by men
cradle of life
now, as it was then
I bow my head
in memory and gratitude
for everyone who bled

## July 2nd

### The Great Divide

how do I cross the great divide
between my life and yours?
I can't begin to comprehend
all your pains and sores
I can promise you
I'll try to do a little more,
because I know our paths were set
by the same eternal hands,
and we both are travelling yet
even though our routes
started long ago and far apart
we can meet together
hand to hand,
and heart to heart

## July 3rd

### Magic Inside

when I was a child
I dreamt I was magic,
descended from
Selkies,
born of the sea
to ride the wind
now,
I remember
my truth
each time
the lightning crashes

## July 4th

Meditate
empty out
all the feelings
all those
thoughts and fears
breathing
in the silence
worry
disappears

## July 5th

Soon,
He'll be too old
to want snuggles
with mom and dad
but for now,
we curl up together
and have our Sunday nap

## July 6th

### Goodbye Kiss

in a constant state of go
yet I'm trying to go slow
hoping the news is just a lie
holding back another cry
trying to think my way through
because there's nothing else to do
I'll keep breathing in and out
even when I'd rather shout
how did the world come to this?
is this it?
blow my dreams a kiss?

## July 7th

### Heavy

weight hangs heavy
on my lids
exhaustion
from carrying the world
like Atlas,
except smaller
I stumble again
then rise up
and step forward
once more

## July 8th

### Rain

the sky
frowned,
then began to fall
against my window
panes,
and all

## July 9th

Early Morning mommy
he comes downstairs
looking for me
worried I've left him
in the night
snuggling up beneath my arm,
I stroke his hair
and in moments,
he's asleep again
safe
in his mother's arms

## July 10th

### Afternoon Nap

another rainy afternoon
but with a view
unlike any other
we crawl into
our sleeping bags,
Chicks 1,2,3,
dad, and mother

## July 11th

### Working Vacation

change is good
the smell of campfires
on the breeze
seeing the mountains
from the other side
feeling the same sun
in a strange place
home is always at hand
when adventure
is in your soul

## July 12th

### Joy

it shows up in small ways
easily missed
if we don't look
like moving your body
to the sound of loons
in the night
closing your eyes
as wind rushes by,
carrying the smell of cedar
as you fall asleep

## July 13th

### Home

coming back,
greeted by indifferent
feline roommates
angry we were gone
at least the house
welcomed us home

## July 14th

NOISY LITTLE BIRDS
fighting in my yard
no one willing to yield
or throw in the last card
my cat watches with delight
and I worry for the crowd
luckily, the window's closed—
so they continue being loud

## July 15th

### Rage

rage is a river
molten and deep
bubbling up
waking the vessel
from sleep
it hurts not the ground
it's poured on
but tastes like acid
until the last drop is gone

## July 16th

TIME NEVER WAITS

grains
slipping
through my hand
I watch the world
turn again
as my tears
drench
the land

## July 17th

### Stress Filled

where is stress carried
what compartment
do we keep it locked in
away from the sun,
blacker than sin?
maybe we breathe it
from inside and out
until it bubbles over
and erupts with a shout

## July 18th

### Freedom

the winds of freedom
rage
blowing across my soul
wiping away
sadness
dissolving
indecision
scouring the fragments
until the edges
shine

## July 19th

### Shine

breathing deep
crisp morning air
summer skies
brilliant blue
watch me run free
without care

## July 20th

### The Day Ahead

what will today bring?
one just never knows
when you expect one thing
the starting line is moved
and away it goes
to another new target,
another kind of goal
one thing I know
deep down, in my soul
is that everything I do
and everything I've done
I'll be able to live with
at the setting of the sun

## July 21st

### Parting Ways

the stone of goodbye
pushes me down
stealing my breath
days ending,
friends parting
every new journey
begins with a farewell
and the hope
for brighter days
slightly tarnished
by the tang
of bittersweet regret

## July 22nd

### Best Intentions

today I will sit down
and write for awhile
stop making excuses
turn off social media,
and smile
I'll craft something
lovely,
witty,
maybe even
a little smart
but first I'll finish my coffee—
because I'll need energy to start

## July 23rd

### Before the Storm

air hangs
dark,
humid,
and rich
smelling of rain
covering the earth
like the finest silk

## July 24th

### Gus

my dog's in love with shoes
and no matter what I do
he eats the insoles,
backings, and glue
even though I tell him no
I feel that's half the fun
you see he likes when
we chase him—
because that's when he knows
his work is done

## July 25th

### Goals

in a contemplative mood
I watch the sun as it rises
the same goal every day
so far, without surprises
so why is it I can't see the way
past, around, or through?
my short term goals fall away
but the long ones never do

## July 26th

### Uncertainty

the future stretches out
unknown and exhilarating
and for one brief,
sparkling moment,
freedom sings a siren song
but before too long
uncertainty whispers,
pulling me back
to the worries of the day
covering me once more
in the soft,
grey blanket
of restlessness again

## July 27th

### Dreamscape

dreams are a reflection of reality
twisted at the seams
sometimes gloriously happy,
at others filled with screams
as my mind tries to process
it smashes life into something new
maybe it isn't happening,
or perhaps...
it's what's really true

## July 28th

### Simple

if a simpler life
is what we say
we want
why do we fill it up
with excess
trying to make up
for what we perceive
we lack?

## July 29th

### Heat Wave

I lay there,
wishing the fan spun faster
as heat covered me
in the night
uncertain if I'd slept at all
on waking,
the morning air heavy
as if someone had pulled
a warm blanket tight

## July 30th

### Tigers

life keeps changing
brightly dangerous
and unknown
out of my element,
suddenly,
I'm thrown
tiger's teeth in the dark
will they leap
and devour me whole?
or will they walk,
purring at my side
until I reach my
unseen goal?

## July 31st

### Sepia Photographs

road trip to the past
and future?
visits with the cousins,
life at a slower pace
summertimes of childhood;
lessons at the pool,
running in the trees,
days stretching out forever
soft summer breezes
leave kisses on my cheeks

CHAPTER NINE

# 

August 1st

AUGUST ARRIVED,
looking quite perplexed
the world seems like it's on fire—
in reality and in text
the year's half over
but something new happens every day
August looked to July for answers
but they had nothing left to say
so taking a deep breath
August held her chin up high
rolling up her sleeves to work,
jealous of the now retiring July

## August 2nd

### Are We There Yet?

so excited to be on a trip
he asked every five minutes
"are we there yet?"
and, despite my irritation,
I considered the simple innocence
of my child's anticipation
of Candy Land
appearing around every corner
when did I lose that joy?
and more importantly,
how does one ever get it back?
meanwhile the road stretched on,
as endless as the prairie sky

## August 3rd

### Homestead

It's late,
and I'm tired
Watching the kids swim
was almost as tiring
as doing it myself
full of too many cookies
and laughter with family,
we curl up
in the beds of my youth,
falling asleep content
a day full of adventures
and time well spent

## August 4th

### Crossroads

Wouldn't it be nice
if right
was easy to find
instead of waiting
at a deserted crossroads,
covered by fog
in a place
you've never been?

## August 5th

### Mirages

down the rabbit hole
familiar,
but decades removed
memories
of days long past
just another mirage,
a simple oasis
in the sky
or a vision
of a new future?

## August 6th

### Chrysalis

weights pull my
eyelids down
I fall asleep,
cocooned
in my safe nest
tomorrow
I'll wake
refreshed
a butterfly
stretching my wings
I'll take to the sky

## August 7th

### Thunderbird Dances

across endless
prairie skies
bringing exhilarating
change
I dream of fighting
side by side,
upholding what is right
beating back those
willing to drag humanity
down
into the endless night

## August 8th

### Kids in a Car

no one drives you as crazy
as kids locked in the car
whether one hour or many
it always feels too far
Lord, grant me some serenity
before I blow my stack
I'm not sure I've got the patience
to last until we're back

## August 9th

Home sweet home
there's no place like home
where your bed is your friend
no road is too long
with your own pillow at the end
when your cats come to greet you
you've possibly been missed
tonight I turned off the lights,
certain I've been blessed

## August 10th

### Reset

Today I'll realign my goals
with my hopes and dreams
reevaluate my priorities
rip caution at the seams
the paradox of choice
won't hold me back anymore
I'll chart a brand new course
and forget about the score
and maybe tonight
when I curl up to go to sleep
I'll drift dreamlessly for once
my promises to myself I'll keep

## August 11th

### Martyr

yesterday he died
serving others until the end
the reasons why are ashes,
and will never make up
for the loss of such a friend
how can we heal others
when we're breaking down inside?
when we're sacrificed for nothing,
then told we're not
even worth the price
wandering in a desert
of lies and his despair
forty years of this
is far too long to bear

## August 12th

### Future Forward

the future is wide open
a field waiting
to be walked
skies yet to be viewed
people with whom
I haven't talked
so, do I turn
and look back,
risk becoming
a pillar of salt?
or do I let the wind
carry me on,
and in uncertainty
exalt?

## August 13th

### Nightmares

sometimes,
the monsters
know my name
other times,
they wear my face
swirling
in my unconscious
they rise,
impossible to kill
until I break free
and awaken,
the last woman standing

## August 14th

### Tenth Anniversary

What makes a decade
more precious than a year
its just another mark in the sand
written out so clear
laughter and love
children and work
hearth and home
but the biggest perk—
growing old together
and learning each day
what it means to be married
love is more
than what they say

## August 15th

### Unexpected Trip

yesterday my toe
caught an edge
down I went
some instinct told me
to soften and accept
so I rolled,
somersaulting
until the world
stopped spinning
and stood up,
in awe of how going
with the flow
allowed me to take flight
ending up in the place
I was supposed to be
all along

## August 16th

Flight of ideas
my mind is
a wide open field
where ideas
chase butterflies
until it's time
to go home

## August 17th

### My Muse

I'm never alone
with these friends of mine
they tell me their stories
nearly all the time
I try to follow a plot
but they merely laugh
and do whatever they want
on their own behalf
but, one way or another,
the stories still unfurl
as much a surprise to me
as any other boy or girl

## August 18th

### Summer's Goodbye

Crickets sing
a farewell song
as fall's icy fingers
stretch out
beaten back—
for now—
by the fading
light of dawn

## August 19th

### Dog Days

one last inferno
as summer
makes its long goodbye
languishing
beside the pool
the grass
begins to die

## August 20th

### Memories of Harvest

Sirius is in the sky
bringing in the hay
harvest on the table
and I'm dreaming of the day
when we worked together
picking apples, beans, and corn
longing for the past
so early on an August morn

## August 21st

### Waiting

standing
in limbo
preparing
for the chips
to fall
I reach out
to grab them
and find
nothing
there at all

## August 22nd

### Fall of Atlantis

Did they know
they were destined
to be a warning and a lesson?
or were they too busy fighting
to see what was on the horizon?
I watch the clouds billowing
and, fearing the future,
I wonder
am I Cassandra,
or Chicken Little?
I hope,
more than anything,
we still have time to change

## August 23rd

### Fall Mornings

Sunday morning dawning
a chill is in the air
pink and coral growing
leaves falling
without a care

## August 24th

### Monday

Monday's here again,
feeling all put out
people groan
when she passes by
causing her to pout

## August 25th

### Favourite Things

early morning memories
of coffee, tea, and love
reading books by the fire
gifts sent from up above

## August 26th

Fall approaches
darker mornings
and chill breezes
make me wonder
how fast could I run
without the stones
that hold me down

## August 27th

### Prime Time

the waiting game is murder;
or so the crows believed
as they sat beside the little house
watching for the package to be received
there inside the cozy little place
a family waited and stewed
until the postman finally came
and happiness ensued

## August 28th

### Friday

Monday's little sister
someone everyone loves—
except the weekend shifters
she's so pretty,
fun and alive
of all the workdays,
the most anticipated of the five
but when Friday comes around,
I try to play it cool
I haven't managed to win her yet
since I met her back at school
and even though
she can't be caught
I'm always happy to see her—
after the week her siblings wrought

## August 29th

### Night visits

somewhere in my dreamscape
people come and go
sometimes they stop
and stay awhile,
but others,
they just flow
no one's ever truly gone
not when they stop by
in my dreams
they still exist
until the end of night

## August 30th

### Back to School

winds swirl the leaves
freshly fallen from the trees
fat flies buzzing lazily
observing all the bees
days are getting shorter
nights become more cool
children ever anxious
at going back to school
parents watch with eyes
bittersweet and lovingly regret
thinking of those summer days
they won't soon forget

## August 31st

### The Last Day

change blows in
but what the future holds
is so uncertain
we take deep breaths,
and facing forward
hand in hand,
we carry on
ready to face the
next curtain

CHAPTER TEN

# September 2020

## September 1st

FRESH START
crisp air
breathing together,
horizons we share

## September 2nd

Somehow,
it's Wednesday,
and my goals
are out of reach
too many priorities,
I should focus on one
yet,
each time I try
something else
has to be done
my list gets longer
as I try in vain
to hold back the sun

## September 3rd

### Little boys

two little boys
snuggled up tight
sleeping beside me
in the early morning light
soft and warm
not yet playful and loud
I cherish the moments
where sleep has them bowed
I know before long
they'll scamper and play
but this soft start with love
is the best part of my day

## September 4th

### The bad sleep

I've reached the age
where it's possible
to wake up more sore
from sleeping funny
than I did climbing the mountain
where Moses
received the commandments
welcome to middle age
my neck seems to say
while the pillow stares
innocently back

## September 5th

### Family tattoo

I'll keep them in
my heart forever
there's nothing more
I need to do
but just to show
the world my love
today
I got something new

## September 6th

### Fractured Time

trying to squeeze life
into the cracks
makes nothing
fit quite right

## September 7th

### It's All Happening At The Zoo

his excitement is so big I smile
as he anticipates a day at the zoo
he can't wait to watch the meerkats,
and maybe see a tiger, too
I snuggle him a bit closer,
wishing I could capture this joy
and keep these memories for ever
my innocent and happy little boy

## September 8th

### Stopwatch

I dream of planting a garden
I can grow with,
books, pianos, and yarn
cats cuddled by the fire,
listening to my attempts
at learning other languages
time to read,
and sit,
and ponder
to have the time
to spend it where I wish,
throw away the stopwatch,
that is true freedom—
living by the sun
and moon
and whims

## SEPTEMBER 9TH

### COMPARISON

that heart-stopping moment
when someone else
wears your favourite item
better than you

## September 10th

### Early Mornings with Gus

earlier each day
the morning arrives
bringing coffee
(at least two cups before five)
with so much to do
and far too little time
I rush from the second
I hear that tiny chime
my internal monitor
is better than any alarm
even if it long ago
lost all of it's charm
at least I have a friend
who sits with me each day
giving me loving licks
without much to say

## September 11th

SHARING THE LOAD
when heaviness
drags me down
into the depths
a memory from beyond
calls to me
tells me
there's life out there
a place where struggles
are soothed
loads are shared
sunny days yet rise
offering its hand
like an old friend,
reminding me
of my why

## September 12th

### Journaling

changes are challenging
life can be so hard
the grass is so much greener
in someone else's nice backyard
the work may be difficult
but it's worth it every time
I have to remind myself of this
in verse, and in rhyme
but somehow it gets easier
when I write it down
as the removal from my head
creates a smile out of my frown

## September 13th

### Strive

eternally seeking,
like a shark in the ocean,
or a collie herding sheep
climbing mountains
on a notion,
fording the next stream
goals challenge us,
keep moving us forward
until one day,
we reach our dreams

## SEPTEMBER 14TH

### THE SHORTEST LIVED GLASSES

Monday's child
was super cute
wearing his brand-new specs
he put them down
for one single moment
—and instantly,
the dog them did wreck

## September 15th

### Stand

when knowing isn't enough
and it's time to take a stand
that's when you must stay strong
and play against the band
marching to the beat
of a slightly different drum
you've always got your own back
when you stand against the sun

## September 16th

### A Productive Morning

Early mornings make long days
but when I can't fall back to sleep
I count my chores one by one
instead of silly sheep
I get up and knock them off
instead of tossing and turning
long before the sun even thinks
about getting burning
then,
when nighttime falls again at last,
I fall into bed asleep,
faster than you can say fast

## September 17th

### Crickets

crickets sing in the early morn,
bravely chirping their way to fall
they will grow silent again
when winter comes to call
but in the stillness,
they bravely shout
uncaring their time has almost come
I wonder how can they ignore
the slowly waning summer sun

## September 18th

### Sam

today is a special day
eight years ago,
I fell in love again
with the tiniest little girl
eyes as big
as her personality
even then,
she was standing up
for herself
firm in her mind
on the way things should be
our littlest hobo forever,
my sweet Sammy

## September 19th

### Cards on the Table

our lives unfold
a hand of cards
dealt by all-seeing hands
tragedy and triumph
no one gets away free
so we hold on
at the table of life
able to see our hand
one card at a time
convinced someone
will win the pot
but life,
as in poker
uses the house deck
and the dealer
wins them all

## September 20th

Time on a dime

so many moments
twist on a dime
unique yet eternal
time after time
every breath in
also must come out
a soul is forever
of that,
I've no doubt

## September 21st

### The Difficult One

sometimes I wonder
what's it's like
to be able to
ride the waves with others,
go with the crowd
into the bright sunshine
but for better or worse,
I'm not built to fit in
walking to the whistle
of my own ideas,
never quite sure
if what I'm doing is correct,
yet unable to change
or be anything else,
I remain apart

## September 22nd

### Forever Love

fatigue at the end of the day
coloured by love and regret
knowing the way the chips will fall
saying nothing, no, not yet
to those who can not listen
what good is prophesy?
or watching others at the dance
for those who can not see?
and yet, the music still plays on
for brothers, sisters, and friends
I'll keep you within my heart
until the time we meet again

## September 23rd

### Aftermath

stunned disbelief
a goal finally found—
six months overdue
joy inflates
like a balloon
a small pop,
air comes rushing through

## September 24th

### Goals

pledged anew,
my energy is rising
night falls around me
I watch the far horizon
time winds down
as the sun dips lower
the sky catches fire
allowing life to move slower
waiting on the cusp
of what will become the future
believing anything is possible
with faith as my only suture

## September 25th

### Where Do I Begin

so much left
to be done
so much
not yet begun
a drop in the ocean
I am overwhelmed
by each and every notion

## September 26th

### The Cure-all

the sickening feeling
of things left undone
wondering what you said
impending doom at the horizon
relieved in one shining moment
by a simple outstretched hand
knowing someone is there
with you,
until the end
together, we are stronger
together, no horizon is too far
together, there is nothing
we cannot overcome

## September 27th

### Fall Sunday

the smell of leaves drifting
through sunshine
holding on
children run,
gleeful as they chase each other
rolling through golden dry grass
spring and fall
unite at last

## September 28th

### After the Alarm

Monday morning rush
waking up after
the alarm
the house is frantic,
out of step—
hope no one
comes to harm!

## September 29th

### The Way it is

some days
things don't go your way
your toast falls
butter-side down,
every light turns red
when you're five minutes late
but some days,
the sun shines more brightly
old friends and laughter
light your way
and you fall asleep
secure
in the arms of love

## September 30th

### Adventures Await

tomorrow
is another adventure
today
is full of change
yesterday's
memories
are ready
to rearrange

# CHAPTER ELEVEN

# October 2020

ctober 1st

The longest day—
with the sweetest smiles
a little further out of the way
but love gives you fuel for miles

## October 2nd

### Molasses

Time is molasses
both sticky and sweet
sometimes too fast
when loved ones we meet
but usually molasses
slows down in the cold
maybe I'm molasses too—
otherwise,
I'm simply getting old!

## October 3rd

### On the Move

Heading out again
into the great wide blue
reversing course knowing
it's the next best thing to do
yet, I'm left wondering
does the universe have a plan?
and if so, will I learn it
before the day I make
my own last stand?

## October 4th

### Ten year plan

what happens when
your ten year plan
is set on fire?
road blocks
and limits
vanish
the sky
is clear ahead
and open highways
lead to a future
beyond
imagination

## October 5th

### My Guys

watching my boys play
giggles from big and small
just like his daddy,
they've both won
my heart and all

## October 6th

New horizons
an old familiar rush
of doing a job
that matters
holding other's hands
keeping safe what shatters
being in the moment
when all is said and done
human meeting human
remembering
we are one

## October 7th

### On call

absence makes the heart grow fonder
as the silence begins to grow
a few moments away from them
and one thing for sure I know
I miss them in the morning
and also in the night
but it's easier to stay away
when I'm doing
what I know is right

## October 8th

What if?
what if one day
I didn't blink?
lived every minute
and didn't stop to think
about the weights
around my neck
or negative thoughts
and said, "what the heck?"
then played in the sun
just like a kid
and all the bad
got up and hid
that day could be
just up ahead
but for now,
I'll make a wish
and go back to bed

## October 9th

### Possibility

They say the prairies
made the best sailors
as farmers
marched off to sea
staring at the fields again,
I see the ocean
in these possibilities

## October 10th

### Thanksgiving Weekend

The familiar smells
fall leaves crisp underfoot
mist kisses my face as
winter knocks on the door
fall puts harvest on the table
a time for family
and giving thanks
before soft blankets
cover the world once more

## October 11th

### The Offer

somewhere between
here and then
the road tried to take
my heart away
swaying in the breeze
the trees almost seemed to say,
"Who needs to have
a house and home,
when you could stay
right here?"
it was easy to turn
the offer down—
after twelve hours
spent on my rear

## October 12th

One more day
to get things done
a long weekend is meant
for more than merely fun
but somehow these Mondays
always disappear
I'll try to be happy
it was ever here

## October 13th

### Monday Tuesday

A Monday Tuesday falls
so far from a happy day
flat grey clouds
do nothing much
to keep my cares away
payment for the weekend
and its longer than usual length
I raise my mug
to the sky above
for coffee,
which gives me strength

## October 14th

### First Snow

people rushing
stop to stare
a little girl squeals
soft cold fluff
on her nose
for one moment,
the world
holds
its breath

## October 15th

### Long Goodbyes

two weeks
enough time
to climb a mountain
canoe a river
harvest the fields
long enough,
but still so short
how do you
say goodbye?

## October 16th

### Sleeping Angels

did the universe ever make
something more beautiful
than the face
of a child sleeping
content
in God's grace?

## October 17th

### Morning Rises

silences breathes in
the early morning light
inhales the sun,
and blows out
the candle
of the night

## October 18th

### Dusty

on her perch
she watches us all
a mountain cat,
too tough to fall
refusing each
and every attempt
at cajoling,
watching our efforts
with great contempt
but when she hears
food's familiar sound
at she last deigns
to hit the ground

## October 19th

### What Matters Most

we all pay the piper
in energy or time
cash is a memory,
only a figment of mind
so be careful
what you spend
constructs aren't real
and nothing in life
is as priceless
as what we choose to feel

## October 20th

### Light of day

I saw the light this morning
shining through the pane
it woke me up slowly
but it didn't land in vain
it spoke of a brighter future
and all I had to do
was put one foot
in front of the other
and smile
as I broke on through

## October 21st

### Busy Brain

buzz, buzz, buzz
busy little brain
not sure how you put
all these new thoughts
upon this train
just when I think
I've got it all figured out
you jump off the tracks
without a doubt

## October 22nd

### Goodbyes

faces I'll remember
long after I'm gone
moments so touching
and sometimes
too hard won
together we've built bridges
climbed mountains
and so much more
at least goodbye
is a thing worth
crying for

## October 23rd

### The Last Week

I'm standing
right at the end
change is here,
seams start to rend
I'll build anew
on solid ground
where my heart
will be safe and sound
and there I'll spread
my wings and fly
underneath
a wide prairie sky

## October 24th

### Snowy Saturday

small moments
on a snowy Saturday
time spent with my kids
warm hugs and hot cocoa—
the best a life can give

## October 25th

### Façade

two more months
until Christmas
with Halloween
nowhere to be seen
snow covers the ground
but masks are evergreen

## October 26th

### Strength

as I sit here by myself
in the early morning dawn
a soft voice calls from within,
saying nothing has gone wrong
because even in the strangest times
you're never really alone
any time you close your eyes
you can find your way back home

## October 27th

### Technology

technology bites the hand
that flips the switch
you think you know
what you're about
until you become its...
which way is this heading?
I only wish I knew
because just when I become
accustomed to it
there's something else
I'm supposed to do

## October 28th

Butterflies of change

that old feeling is back
butterflies
in my throat
they tickle
as they choke
and take
my breath away

## October 29th

### Last Day

just like every other day
I'll have some coffee,
putting myself through
one foot at a time
all the while trying
not to think about
the mountains
I've yet to climb

## October 30th

### At Sea

waking up to an emptiness
where my purpose used to be
startled by the changes
I feel a little out at sea
I'm sure it will settle in—
if I only give it time
but right now,
at this moment,
there's nothing I can do
but rhyme

## October 31st

### Halloween

all the ghosts of my past,
goblins of fear and dread
come slinking out this Halloween
and go marching through my head
because skeletons need a closet,
they wanted to stay at home
but they were dragged out anyway
led by the beat of a heart—
probably, my own
just like any other magic
the true power comes from within
this Halloween is no different
as the players wink and grin

CHAPTER TWELVE

# November 2020

ovember 1st

Beginning and End

twelve hours,
three kids
two cats and a dog
too much chocolate
Halloween spent on the road
arriving to greet family
home at last

## November 2nd

### Memories and Moving

too many items in search
of a new place to be
just when I think
it would be easy to start over,
fresh and new
tiny handprints catch my eye,
a favourite mug reminds me
of early morning coffee on the couch
and I smile,
gently placing the books
back on the bookshelf

## November 3rd

### The Best Nest

discoloured purple and blue
I'm heavy in my bones
from the stacks of books
and a few actual sticks and stones
I've moved in with my brood,
and built my little nest
now I must feather it just so
knowing that,
with a little love,
it'll look it's very best

## November 4th

### Gone

another long day
no longer at home
in this empty house
gone are the hopes
and life
instead,
an empty shell remains,
ready for someone else
to build their dreams anew

## November 5th

### House and Home

I would drive 1000 miles
to make a house a home
I'd say goodbye
to all I've known
so that I never more
shall roam

## November 6th

### Home

first nights
different sounds
new shadows
on the walls
but the same small bodies
tucked in with love
together
under the same roof
we're home again
at last

## November 7th

### Beginnings

today was backbreaking
soul shaking,
heart mending,
beginnings ending,
time for love
and peace
from above
today,
when darkness falls
true character calls

## November 8th

### Possibilities

looking around
the stacks of odds and ends
I envision what will be
pieces of my old life
scattered
and out of place
waiting for me
to set things right

## November 9th

### Snow day

they called for a snow day
and when the townsfolk got the news
the children danced and sang,
while the parents
may have hit the booze

## November 10th

### Change

I can move mountains
if I want
one stone at a time
isn't too tough
the same is true for change—
one small smile
can often be enough

## November 11th

### Remembrance

They were young,
barely out of childhood
when they made their stand
told it was their duty,
and they were doing good
so they marched off to war
in twos and also threes
but often died alone
whether or not they pleased
eyes open or closed
we all walk through the door
where we will be reunited
for ever and once more

## November 12th

### The Glue

even when separated
by time and space,
we stick together
nothing can erase
the glue of memory
and of love
stronger than fear or anger
sent from up above

## November 13$^{th}$

### Friday the 13th

will this Friday the 13th
end in fire or in snow?
or will it just fall asleep—
it depends on where you go
in my own cozy corner
I'll crawl back into bed
tomorrow is Saturday
so maybe I'll sleep late instead

## November 14th

### Saturday and the Cake

I had such big plans
until that cake called my name
it whispered to me "it's Saturday"
(as if that absolved it from any blame)
I tried to resist,
because the older I get
the more it stays with me
the calories linger twice as long,
and the heartburn an eternity
the migraine party is no fun
the solution to this problem
is easy, tried, and true—
stop making cakes and icing
but alas,
that's too hard for me to do!

## November 15th

### Home Sweet Home

halfway through another month
the time has flitted past
I've cooked,
and cleaned,
and organized
to make this nest my last
and while I say that every time
this one will be 'It'
I'm sure
because this house
will be a home
with family
as the special cure

## November 16th

### Stress Baking

when cooking becomes a problem
you know you're in the soup
I baked two dozen granola bars,
lemon potatoes,
and fish to boot!
but when I eyed the pantry
for something new to make
it was time to put the mixer down
before I made a culinary mistake

## November 17th

### Morning Thoughts

in the very early mornings
it's nice having extra time
to sit and sift through my thoughts
(often, they come out in rhyme)
the animals sleep beside me,
and I'm sure they agree I'm strange
but, better they think I'm crazy
than for me to have no time
to ponder my life and change

## November 18th

### Big Dreams

In my dreams
I glimpse the truth
as varied and strange
as it may be
hidden in macabre
and twisting paths
if I can only understand
it will set me free

## November 19th

### Silence in the Noise

the rush of a day's work done,
kids talking at once
to be heard first
so loud,
yet a sweeter sound
(other than silence)
has never existed
as diametrically opposed
as the sun and stars
each beautiful
in their own way
and never
to be taken for granted

## November 20th

### Black Friday

Next week is Black Friday
I guess?
I get confused
by all the mess
I'm not American
so there's that fact
but the concept strikes me
as too abstract
how is it that shopping
became a thing
in a time meant for family,
food, and carolling?
I guess I may never know
so I'll stay at home
and watch it snow

## November 21st

### Snow and Cookies

fresh snow
leads to cold noses
warmed by sugar cookies
"Save some for Santa"
are the last words said
before calm
descends again
leaving snow puddles
at the door,
shining in the sun

## November 22nd

### Time Flys

where does all
the time go?
does it flutter away
like the snow?
or does it sneak
and slide right by
in the twinkling
of an eye?
Sunday night
is here again
I take a breath,
pause,
and let a new week
waltz right in

## November 23rd

### Truth in Dreams

dreams show us things
our minds can't explain
during the bright of day
at night,
truths that can break bones,
steal the breath from our lungs,
break or mend your heart
come strolling out
prepackaged in chunks of the bizarre,
bits of shimmering sugar
sprinkled on top
to make them easier to swallow
and forget
moments after the sand
leaves your eyes

## November 24th

### Seeing Clearly in 2020

One month until Christmas, but nothing feels the same.

People are snug in their houses or work, keeping to themselves the rest of the time. Normally, the rounds of parties would be headache-inducing, similar to the scheduling Tetris we do at work when we're short-staffed.

I would already be starting to feel burned out trying to keep up, but this year, the world has fallen silent even as holiday decorations quietly deck the halls of our individual dwellings.

We know the holidays will be different this year.

Quarantines and masks are the new must-have accessories for the season, and there's a feeling of something I can't describe in the air at odds with the usual season's greetings.

Looking for meaning, and a way to describe how I feel, I eventually stumbled across a word that fit.

*Hiraeth—*

> *A Welsh word, used to describe a sensation of homesickness and grief mixed with a longing for the departed, for homeland, or the romanticized past.*

In many ways, I think we are all feeling *hiraeth* for 2019 and how life is/was supposed to go.

We had a sense of certainty about what life was but then, as if mocking our smugness, along came the pandemic.

2020 has been a year of struggle for people everywhere.

Lost loved ones, lost jobs, lost labours of love and creativity.

Friends and family told to keep six feet apart.

The terror of making a vulnerable loved one sick without knowing.

Children lost schooling, and went virtual.

Classrooms of technology abound now in a way never before seen for people of all ages and educational levels.

Families lost the chance to say goodbye, and were devastated to watch loved ones passing away via technology, or worse, hear it from a stranger dressed in an isolation-type space suit instead of through kisses and hugs and the usual bedside vigils that can bring at least a semblance of closure.

I have been witness to these changes.

Shifts of seismic nature as we stand at ground zero and hope we don't fall.

I've been luckier than so many, but that didn't keep change from my doorstep. I moved over a thousand kilometres away, started a new job, and uprooted my family to be closer to my extended relatives.

We may have escaped illness so far, but not the changes the pandemic brought to our world.

I believe we don't always have the ability to choose what happens to us in life, but that doesn't mean we have no power. We can always choose what we do with the hand we've been dealt.

Perhaps it's that pesky midlife crisis I've read so much about.

Or, perhaps it's the *hiraeth* making me long for a simpler time.

Either way, this year has altered how I view the world, and encouraged me to choose differently.

With life changing around us in ways we can't control, 2020 has simplified life almost as much as it complicated it.

In a time of stark and sometimes enforced isolation, I chose the closeness of family, even if we can't physically be together.

I chose to simplify at a time where life reminded us what truly matters and what is the mere busywork of modern life we've become distracted by.

When 2020 started, seeing clearly was the goal, the theme word for the year I wanted to work toward.

Despite the reality of what happened, and even though this year didn't go at all the way I intended, in many ways, it still ended up being a year of seeing clearly.

But man, what a difference a year can make!

## November 25th

### Night Settles

empty of thought,
alone in the dark
at last I breathe in,
and let the day out
peace descends
in snow-covered blankets
while the moon winks
goodnight to the stars

## November 26th

### Drama King

the proudest being in the house
a cat amongst the kittens
he's the loudest in the jungle
(even when he hasn't lost his mittens)
heaven forbid you pat him
when he doesn't want your touch
but if you stop before he's done
he'll meow and meow too much!

## November 27th

### Sunrise Salutations

I'll give an early morning thanks
for waking up today
even when my body hurts—
and is that another grey?
I know I am truly blessed
each time I open my eyes
and have a chance see the world
lit by a beautiful sunrise

## November 28th

### Humanity is Pain

bittersweet and sharp,
pain of goodbyes
or one perfect moment
touching nature's last sunrise
the agony of loss,
the beauty of true love found
ache of growth and death,
burying priceless treasures
in the cold hard ground
perfection, triumph,
and even, sometimes, mirth
twists and turns as they mix
and in the end,
pain can create rebirth

## November 29th

### First and last

the last day before another first
like a shark that never grows old
I keep moving on
until I can finally catch on,
and hold
it's funny how each time
I think there's nothing new
life flips the table
and gives me something else to do
I can only shake my head
as I look to the sky above
believing there's a bigger plan
fuelled by the greatest power—
love

## November 30th

### Back in the Saddle

It's time to get back in the saddle,
jump right into the show
a schedule looms in front of me
and I know which way to go
the path may still be murky
and rocks litter the way
but at least I've got a direction
and a place I'm going today

CHAPTER THIRTEEN

# December 2020

ecember 1st

Last Month

first of another long month,
but the last one of the year
people are tired and hurting
and the world seems to live in fear
but I think the sky is beautiful
every time I go for a walk
and conversation feels more precious
when you finally get a chance to talk
it's true this year wasn't expected
but really—what year ever is?
so I'll take a moment to be grateful
for the things I never thought I'd miss

## December 2nd

### Health and Blessings

the greatest gift of all
is when people trust
that we won't fall
that answers exist
for us to give
our best we can
so that they live

## December 3rd

### Winter Morning Battle

winter darkness
fills my bones
making them heavy as lead
my alarm clock wages
an uphill war
as I fight to stay
tucked in bed

## December 4th

### Comfort Zone

my comfort zone
is never far
from home
and the warmth
of those
who chose
to love me most
even in
my darkest hour
I can feel
love's amazing power
to raise me up
from the deepest well
straight to heaven
and out of hell

## December 5th

### Pizza Coma

it's later than I'd like
for my stomach
to be so full
the pizza was
delicious
and dessert was
hard to pull
myself away
from the table
to go lay down
now I'm ready for bed
too content
to even frown

## December 6th

### Impatience

why is there never
enough time
to do the things I'd like?
my wheels are stuck
and the engine revs in neutral
broken have-to's
clutter the highway
and daylight fades
on another mile
in the rear view window

## December 7th

### Fur-ball

as small as my palm
it's little heartbeat fluttered
deceptively strong
before I knew what hit me
I was wrapped around
its tiny paw
the little kitty fur-ball
burrowed stealthily
into my heart

## December 8th

"But we've only just started!"
he complains,
when life intrudes
on his special time
I know,
little one
I feel the same way
but I always carry you
with me,
in my heart,
no matter how far apart
we are in the day

## December 9th

### Low Pressure Blues

eyelids
grow heavy
clouds start
their deluge
I have a magic power;
feeling low pressure systems
ensue

## December 10th

### So this is Christmas

Christmas looks different this year
than how we hoped it would
we've been told to stay apart—
for the greater good
and even though I know
the reasons why I will
I'll miss my loved ones desperately
to keep them from being ill
but while we have to stay apart
this time won't last forever
once things calm down a bit
we'll be healthy again—
together

## December 11th

### Lightness

feeling buoyant is the best—
even more so
early in the day
starting with a crisp,
clear morn
running on an icy way
nothing beats the feeling
of breathing in the cold
feet shuffling so slow
yet today,
I don't feel as old

## December 12th

### Balance

standing on a teeter-totter,
knowing one step
either way
and everything collapses
holding on
I keep the plates
spinning
while I smile
for the crowd,
and lift my chin
a little higher

## December 13th

### Odd Thoughts

even numbers seem safer
than ones that are a little odd
and yet in my life, at least
they're where I most
feel the presence of God
the universe sometimes whispers
its precious secrets to me
and if I listen hard enough
I can peek at what will be
momentous occasions
decorate the fabric of my life
but for some reason it seems
that most of my strife
has landed on the evens,
both the amazing and the bad
so here's hoping this season
will be more boring than sad
and that 2021 ushers in
a quiet, odd little year
to let us pick up the pieces,
sit with friends,
and enjoy a nice cold beer

## December 14th

### Facebook Feed

memories appear
on my social media feed
of my life, then and now,
and I simply must agree
although things have changed
and feel tougher every day
there's nothing I'd trade
to go back there and stay
things were different then,
I'm not the same little girl
now I'm a grown woman,
living in a complex world
it's not always perfect
but I know that's quite okay
because beauty is something
I've learned to see along the way

## December 15th

### Christmas Prep

stolen moment
stocking stuffers
presents wrapped
on the sly
little ones
are shooed away
while mommy
encourages dreams to fly

## December 16th

### Cats in Capes

minutes are as odd
as cats wearing capes
they care not
for your opinion
while they sit
staring you
in the face

## December 17th

### A week until Christmas

one week until Christmas
and threats are in full bloom
getting children to listen
is nigh impossible without zoom
I remind them Santa
can decide not to come—
temporarily, it halts all fighting
(okay, only some)
one week until Christmas
and tomorrow school is out
I'm grateful I'm still working
so I won't hear them shout

## December 18th

Organizing myself has been
on my list now for awhile
It seemed insurmountable
so I put it off,
with a sheepish smile
but time is running out—
now it's only weeks away
the day many have prayed for—
the end of 2020, hurray!
what will the new year bring?
none of us have a clue
but I'm ready to create my 2021 list
of all the things I have to do

## December 19th

### Raised with Love

all I want for my children
is a piece of land
good solid ground
a footing on which to stand
there I'll grow them
strong and free
surrounded by love
and family
life won't be easy,
there will be ups
and downs
but we'll make
the best of it we can
and always hug away
the frowns

## December 20th

### Christmas Fever Pitch

Christmas season is here
and excitement at its peak
the kids shriek a lot—
at times, I'd like to hide until next week
but just when it feels too much
and I can't bear it anymore
witnessed moments of joy and awe
remind me what I do this for
suddenly, the edge is gone
muting some of their noise
seeing my children happy
is better than a world of toys

## December 21st

### Calm before the Winter

the sky is a
bright white
like seagulls
in full flight
ominously warning
of a storm
we can't yet see
silently above,
now forming
birds fly
far and fast
expecting the winter
now returned
at last

## December 22nd

### Fever Pitch

effervescent
anticipation
bubbles up
again
as the season
comes to life
true magic
lives within

## December 23rd

### Performance Anxiety

everything's changing
again
making me wonder
if I'm doing it right
still hoping I don't
trip and fall
into the blinding
spotlight
and then,
right in the middle
of my doubt
a simple smile
shines,
and lifts me out

## December 24th

The Night before Christmas
'Twas the night before Christmas,
and all through my parents' house,
children were squealing,
full of vinegar and grouse

I had a headache,
as did most of the adults,
from listening to the small ones,
their laughter and their shouts

We played all the carols
and sang with much delight,
after eating a good Ukrainian supper
until our pants were tight

We hung up the stockings
on the arms of the couch
threw the kids into bed
while they tried not to grouch

You see, Santa is coming
and they tried to be good
so off to bed they went
like nice kids should

Mom and Dad will fill up

the stockings over night,
so when the children wake up
they'll be full of such delight

AND I HEARD MYSELF EXCLAIM
as they went off to bed,
I hope Santa brings mommy sleep,
because I'm so tired, I'm half dead

## December 25th

Christmas

the dishes are done,
and I'm full up
to my soul
Christmas memories
are more wonderful
than presents as the goal
the warmth of the season
lasts long after this day
and family is forever
good and bad,
come what may

## December 26th

### Boxing Day Blues

another Christmas
is gone again
presents unwrapped,
bags and boxes
stashed away
to be used once more,
perhaps
leftovers fill empty mouths
the anticipation
all but vanished
as we hover in a week
of in-between
before the old year
is banished

## December 27th

### Clean up

trying to clean up
the after Christmas storm
(known as the ghost of Christmas clutter)
toys, crafts, and wrappings abound
making all the parents shudder
it's funny how much
presents can expand—
what was once in tiny boxes
is now a pile big enough
on which to stand

## December 28th

### Forward Thinking

smack in the middle of a week
nothing special to see or do
I catch myself dreaming ahead
to 2021, and even 2022
with the hopes of yesterday
now in my rear view mirror,
tomorrow waiting out of reach
I wish I saw things clearer
this was going to be the year
where I got my act together
instead it careened wildly for everyone—
the best part was the weather
for now, I'll keep my eyes facing front
and make plans for what's ahead
but fill my checklist with plans a, b, and c
so I can sleep soundly in my bed

December 29th

Planning ahead for 2021

I like to plan out my year before it happens.

There's nothing quite like the anticipation of glorification, don't you agree? We look at all the things we want to do or achieve, and no one plans to fail when we imagine the outcomes we want in our mind's eye.

That future world is one of accomplishment, magic, and all things desired arriving easily on a silver platter. The truth, of course, is most often what I (we) plan doesn't go the way we want.

There's no 76 trombones in a marching band, and hardly any one rolls out a red carpet anymore. But truthfully, that's okay.

My logical side knows the chances of all the things on my list happening are under the 10% line, and dreams the big dreams anyway.

I'm the kid who still lives by the "shoot for the moon and you'll land in the stars" maxim. I guess that makes me an eternal romantic, in the truest sense of the word.

Which leads to the problem I have with attempting to live out my plans. Aiming for that shiny man in the moon is often accompanied by a smidge of lack of focus along with a dash of trouble with follow through, not to mention finding the time to do all the things I'd like.

Maybe it's because I'm moonstruck, but more likely, it's because I work with the end goal in mind, and careen wildly in the general direction instead of taking things one step at a time, or making an actual plan on how to get there.

Basically, I travel life without a road map.

I look at my destination, draw an imaginary line with my finger, say, "I've got it!" and throw the map away.

But I *don't* got it, because five minutes later I forgot where I was going. And since becoming a mother, sometimes what I was doing as well.

Sigh.

This, of course, leads to many interesting journeys, plenty of life experience, and occasionally unexpected fun things happening along the way.

But if you want to get to a *specific* destination, you kind of have to know where to point your vehicle.

I'd like to think I'm getting better at that.

A little.

Maybe.

Those of you who know me in person can think of times I've achieved my goals, but likely twice as many instances where I've said something and haven't followed through.

It's weird, but the big life goals were easier to obtain—due to the well-laid out steps people have to take to get there.

School, university, residency, work, etc.

Check, check, done.

But the dreams I see for the future now are big, nebulous things: simplifying, creating, exploring, becoming.

These goals are hard to break down in the same step-by-step fashion, because there is no one size fits all to get there, and I'm not even sure what that looks like for me at this point.

So, I'm going to try approaching planning differently this year. I'm going to see if I can find a few measurable steps for my pie-in-the-sky goals, then break them down further into more manageable chunks.

You know, the actual SMART goal strategy that has existed a long time. That I haven't ever used because I may be more SMRT.

(Homer Simpson, this one is for you lol.)

I'll still have the massive night sky of dreams to stare at, but I'm curious where I'll end up playing by rules.

Namely, this year I'm going to scale back from the craziness that was 2019 (I think I counted 19 writing projects that were published!) and focus more than I was able to in the never-ending chronic anxiety that 2020 created (where I published a measly two things, and left a bunch of things undone.)

This year, I'll work to finish one book a quarter, and those books are already mapped out. Sadly, I am not mature enough (internally motivated enough?) to do things without deadlines, and external ones still work the best for me.

That means I have three weeks until my next novel, A Destiny Found, will launch on January 18th, 2021 Once that book is up and running, I'll work on setting the next one for early April, and so on.

Of course, that doesn't mean I won't jump ahead, or zig-zag off in another direction entirely, but I'm hoping if I plan out a few basic steps it will force me to work through my dreams.

Even if I don't achieve them all, I'm hoping I won't get lost in confusion like I did in 2020.

So far, it's starting out a little suspect— my 2021 planner is in the mail and may be delayed…

But hey—life is what happens while you're making other plans, after all.

Wish me luck—and I'll wish the same for you!

## December 30th

### Wanderlust

the grass is always greener
in places I've never been
the world is full of wonders
I have never seen
and now I've added lockdown
to having work and kids
it's a wonder parents can survive
without giving into their Ids
I take a few deep breaths
and remind myself
it's not forever
tonight,
we'll do a virtual family trip
on Facebook,
and tour the Rockies
at home together

## December 31st

Tomorrow
anticipation wars
with the ghosts
of yesterday
fresh doubts
are met
with breathlessness
as tomorrow
tiptoes in

# Afterword

It's taken me wayyyy longer to compile this book than I expected.

Part of that was all the emotion going through these entries stirred up. Some made me laugh, many made me cry, but all of them caused me to linger.

In some ways, it felt like I was reviewing an old photo album in words of a time long past. I could remember some of the feelings, but not always the specific details of what was happening when I wrote the daily post.

The people and places were familiar, but not home to my thoughts any longer.

The world has changed since I began to write a daily blog, and so have I.

I'm still creating, but with less free time. Healthcare around the world is in crisis, along with many other institutions, especially education.

We're all feeling overstretched, overtired, anxious, and in many cases, far past burned out.

I believe maintaining a morning poetry practice and posting every day, even when I haven't had time to write the longer pieces I'd like to, has kept me mentally and emotionally in a place where I'm able to continue to provide care.

Honestly, I'm not sure if I would be able to keep showing up for work without it.

I've seen more death in the last three years than the rest of my career put together, but I've also appreciated each sunrise in a way that feels more miraculous as well.

I'm not sure exactly how we'll do it, but I know we will get through this too.

Humans are resilient.

We tell stories, band together, and continue to love each other.

Together, we'll get to a time and place of stability in this new world we're creating.

Right now, with so many people feeling angry and unheard, I've never seen so much internal and external fighting. But I hope that, like with any construction project, this is simply the first step.

We have to tear down the old thing first before we can build up the new and improved version.

Along the way, there are bound to be challenges, but if we keep hoping, dreaming, and most of all, loving each other, I know we'll someday look back and say,

Wow. The journey was rocky, but look at that view.

It was all worth it.

Thank you for coming along with me on my journey through 2020, and as always,

I wish you health, happiness, and love.

*H. M. Gooden*

# About the Author

H. M. Gooden is family physician, wife, and mother who began writing as a way to find light and magic during endless sleepless nights spent raising babies. In addition to narrative non-fiction poetry and prose, she is an international best selling YA fantasy writer.

She can be reached at www.hmgoodenauthor.com

## *Also by H.M. Gooden*

**Non Fiction**

**Passages: Death, Dementia, and Everything in Between**

**What We Bring to the Practice of Medicine: Perspectives from Women Physicians**

**The Rise of the Light Trilogy**

**Dream of Darkness**

**The Stone Dragon**

**The Phoenix and The Witch**

**The Elements of Light**

**(Continuing Adventures from the Rise of the Light)**

**Fiona's Gift** (Prequel to Dream of Darkness)

**Dragons are Forever** (prequel to the Dragons of the North Trilogy, coming soon! )

**Zahara's Quest** (comes after The Raven and Witch Hunter Book 4 chronologically)

**The Raven and The Witch Hunter books**

**The Raven and The Witch Hunter Book 1**

**The Raven and The Witch Hunter Book 2: The Spirit of Big Bear**

**The Raven and The Witch Hunter Book 3: The Wedding**

**The Raven and The Witch Hunter Book 4: Honeymoon and Full Moon Blues**

**The Raven and The Witch Hunter Omnibus: Volumes 2-4**

**The Born of Destiny Series**

**The Lost Soul**

**The Cursed Heart**

**Destiny Found**

**Stand Alone Books and Short Stories**

**Darkness on the Nile**

**I was a Teenage Vegetarian Zombie Detective**

**Mai's First Date**

**To Capture the Heart of Spring**

**Wendigo**

**Seasons of Summerland**

www.ingramcontent.com/pod-product-compliance
Lightning Source LLC
Chambersburg PA
CBHW020147090426
42734CB00008B/723